D1412740

THE MAGIC OF THE MUNROS

IRVINE BUTTERFIELD

DAVID & CHARLES

Page 1: Am Basteir and the Bhasteir Tooth (*John Allen*)
Page 2: Stuchd an Lochain from Sron Chona Chorein (*John Allen*)
Page 4: The Cuillin from Elgol (*Irvine Butterfield*)
Page 5: Looking to Buachaille Etive Mor from the summit of Beinn a' Bhric (*Irvine Butterfield*)
Page 7: The summit of Ben Nevis from Tower Ridge (*John Allen*)

ACKNOWLEDGEMENTS

I would like to thank the many friends and acquaintances without whose assistance this book would not have been created. I am deeply indebted to all who have so generously given of their time, and consider this compilation is as much theirs as it is mine. I therefore acknowledge with gratitude the help and encouragement given by John Allen, Campbell Burnside, Paul Craven, Mike Dales, John Digney, Ian Evans, Allen Fyffe, Don Green, Hamish Lean, Jim Maison, David May, David McLeod, Ian Mitchell, Martin Moar, Lorraine Nicholson, Alan O'Brien, Clarrie Pashley, Keith Pennyfather, John Pringle, Ruaridh Pringle, Stuart Rae, Tom Rix, Iain A. Robertson, Ralph Storer, Jim Teesdale, Adam Watson, Roy Wentworth, Iain White, Peter and Heather Willimot, and Richard Wood.

A DAVID & CHARLES BOOK

First published in the UK in 1999

Copyright © Irvine Butterfield 1999
Paintings © Paul Craven 1999

Irvine Butterfield has asserted his right to be identified as author of this work in accordance with the Copyright, Designs and Patents Act, 1988.

All rights reserved. No part of this publication may be reproduced, stored in a retrieval system, or transmitted, in any form or by any means, electronic or mechanical, by photocopying, recording or otherwise, without prior permission in writing from the publisher.

A catalogue record for this book is available from the British Library.

ISBN 0 7153 0850 5

Book design by Les Dominey Design Company, Exeter
and printed in Hong Kong by Hong Kong Graphic & Printing Ltd
for David & Charles
Brunel House   Newton Abbot   Devon

CONTENTS

INTRODUCTION

'OUR LIFE, EXEMPT FROM PUBLIC HAUNT,

FINDS TONGUES IN TREES, BOOKS IN RUNNING BROOKS,

SERMONS IN STONES, AND GOOD IN EVERYTHING.'

THESE WORDS CONCLUDED THE SHORT PREFACE TO the first *Scottish Mountaineering Club Journal* in which the then Editor stated that it would surprise many of the readers to learn that there were more than 300 mountains in Scotland exceeding 3000 feet. In the following year, 1891, Hugh Thomas Munro, later Sir Hugh Munro of Lindertis, published his *Tables* of the Scottish 3000ft peaks. Commenting upon the work the Editor remarked that 'The immense extent of the labour undertaken by Mr Munro will be apparent even on the most cursory survey of his Tables'. It was thus that the term *Munro's Tables* first entered the mountain lexicon.

Since the Reverend A.E. Robertson first bent to kiss the cairn, and then his wife, on the summit of Meall Dearg of the Aonach Eagach above Glen Coe to celebrate the completion of the first ascent of the mountains listed, the number of hill-walkers seeking to visit the summits of Scotland's 3000ft peaks has accelerated, and are now numbered in hundreds.

Their personal odyssey – for such it should be – takes many forms. The unhurried perambulation of the modest walker may seem to sit at odds with the challenge of completing the round within the shortest possible time, but each have their place in the expanding horizons of the Munroist. Just as those who pursue the sport of 'Munro-bagging' in its various forms, so each and every mountain has its own shape and character.

This may be a finely honed ridge, crag, or the remoteness of a broad rounded hill.

In trying to capture the essence of a particular peak, or the spirit of a day on a chosen hill, the mountain photographer has to contend with the added challenge of the ever shifting light of the seasons. All too often luck plays a part when time, place and people come together. To the cameraman such are moments to savour and record.

It has been a long cherished ambition to put together a volume of images to portray that attraction and mystery of the mountains we have come to know as Munros. They are here regarded as objects of beauty and interest rather than as a mere catalogue of summits to be won.

Friends, old and new, have pursued this particular theme in quest of that special magic of the Munros. In so doing they share some of the joys of these particular peaks. Readers may recall their own pleasures past, or perhaps anticipate the attractions of a chosen hill yet to be visited. The photographic contributors have also responded in no small measure to the appeal of John Muir to 'do something to make the mountains glad', and in so doing have generously given of their energies to help promote the conservation efforts of the John Muir Trust. This is their celebration of the Scottish 3000ft mountains.

IRVINE BUTTERFIELD
Pitcairngreen, Perth

THE SOUTHERN HIGHLANDS

THE SOUTHERN HIGHLANDS ARE AN IDEAL INTRODUCTION TO THE SCOTTISH mountains since for the most part the hills are grass and heather covered. Some of the hills do possess outcrops and steep buttressed slopes but these present few problems as any difficulties encountered are easily by-passed. The proximity to the towns and cities along the Forth-Clyde corridor provided the early pioneers from these conurbations with a ready playground. The pleasures and freedoms enjoyed on these hills were to fire imaginations to seek out the greater ranges to the north.

Left: Schiehallion from Loch Rannoch (*Paul Craven*)

BEN LOMOND

3195ft/974m Beacon mountain

An old Brittonic word 'llumon', or the Gaelic 'laom', a beacon, may well be the source of this mountain's name. Its shape and detached position make it visible from large areas of the Lowlands and thus an ideal height on which to place warning fires to transmit their signal. Its commanding position and commensurate views have nowadays made it a great favourite of Glaswegians who claim it as their own.

The mountain's profile amply illustrates why this mountain has illuminated many a walker's vision to seek further mountains to conquer. A much favoured view of the early pioneers was that from Beinn Narnain, looking across the isthmus between Loch Long and Loch Lomond.

Left: Ben Lomond from slopes of Beinn Narnain (*Tom Rix*)

BEINN NARNAIN

3038ft/926m Mountain of the notches

An early reference to the mountain names it as Ben Varnan. This is most likely from the Gaelic 'bhearnan', notches or gaps, an apt description of the fissured rock beneath the summit.

As one of the 'Arrochar Alps' within easy reach of the Clyde-side conurbations it is a popular outing for a short winter's day. Those out early often combine their ascent with a visit to the tops of the neighbouring Cobbler.

Right: Beinn Narnain from The Cobbler (*Paul Craven*)

BEINN IME

3317ft/1011m Butter mountain

The connection with butter is obscure and the most plausible explanation offered is that a face seamed with the foaming streams after rain runs milky-white. Central and highest of the 'Arrochar Alps' the ascent of this hill is often linked with one of the adjacent peaks to add interest to the mountain day.

BEN VANE

3005ft/916m The middle mountain

Middle because it lies in the centre of the 'Arrochar Alps' between Beinn Ime and Ben Vorlich. One of the lower heights in Munro's list, this hill is rather upstaged by its companions.

Seen from points to the east of Loch Lomond the smaller peak establishes its separate identity

and, with a similar rugged structure, the equal in every respect to the higher Beinn Ime.

Left: Beinn Ime and Ben Vane from Loch Arklet (*David May*)

BEN VORLICH

3094ft/943m Mountain of the bag-shaped bay

There are many suggestions as to the origin of the corrupted word 'vorlich' in the name. Beinn Mhor-Luig, mountain of the big hollow, is appropriate when seen from Ardlui. Beinn Mhor Loch, mountain of the big loch, would also be appropriate given its proximity to Loch Lomond as would Beinn Mhor-leacach, big stony mountain, here suggesting the presence of flat rocks. But it is the presence of the farm of Ardvorlich at the

mountain's foot which provides the best clue, as in translation from ard mhur bhlaig this means 'promontory of the sea-bag' and thereby in turn links the mountain with Loch Lomond.

Many of the features can be seen from the heights immediately to the north so that the many possible interpretations of the name appear in context, be they hollow, bay, or loch.

Left: Ben Lomond and Ben Vorlich from Troisgeach (*Irvine Butterfield*)

BEINN BHUIDHE

3110ft/948m Yellow mountain

The dried grasses and bents gave colour to this great back of a mountain. Easy access is denied so that the long approaches detract from the popularity of this hill. There is a clearer perspective of the mountain's detachment from peaks ranged about it, those to the north hinting at its panoramas of the Clyde estuary and the distant hills of Arran.

Above: Beinn Bhuidhe from Beinn Dubhchraig (*Irvine Butterfield*)

BEINN A' CHLEIBH

3005ft/916m Hill of the chest or creel
The roundness of this hill may look like
an upturned creel, any chest being the
darker recesses of flanking gullies.
Northern and western slopes dense with
conifers detract from any illusions of
grandeur the mountain may entertain, and
overshadowed by the grander Ben Lui it
is regarded by many a mountaineer as a
mere pawn on the chess board of the
Munroist's game.
Left: Beinn a' Chleibh and Ben Lui from
Cruachan access road (*David May*)

BEN LUI

3707ft/1130m Mountain of the calf (young deer)

The calf from the Gaelic 'laogh' can also mean dear one. In the sense that the hill is held in affection this is indeed true as it has always been a winter favourite when a snowy Central Gully is often the chosen ascent.

The entrance to this *couloir* is long anticipated on the long walk up Glen Cononish, the mountain all the while dominant ahead.

Left: Ben Lui from Glen Cononish (*Irvine Butterfield*)

BEN OSS

3376ft/1029m Mountain of the elk

The Gaelic 'os' can mean an elk or loch-outlet. The presence of a tarn and stream bearing the same name suggests that this was a place where the elk was found before it was hunted to extinction.

BEINN DUBHCHRAIG

3209ft/978m Mountain of the black rock

The black rock which gave this mountain character is not a conspicuous feature on the normal route of approach from the north. Appreciation of its rugged qualities requires a long plod across the moors above Glen Falloch and are therefore seldom seen.

On first acquaintance on approaches from the road near Tyndrum the two fuse into the one hill mass and are better judged in their own right as individuals from a higher vantage point across Glen Cononish.

Above: Ben Oss and Beinn Dubhchraig from Beinn Chuirn (*Irvine Butterfield*)

15

An Caisteal

3264ft/995m The castle

A prominent rock near the summit gave this mountain its name and is a useful landmark when seeking to identify the various peaks from the road along Glen Falloch.

Left: An Caisteal from Glen Falloch (*Irvine Butterfield*)

Beinn Chabhair

3061ft/933m Mountain of the hawk

The name must be taken from the older Gaelic 'cabhar' otherwise the alternative 'mountain of the antler' might be appropriate. As the southern outlier of a rugged chain of five mountains above Glen Falloch its natural route of ascent starts near the old coaching inn at Inverarnan to which many of its visitors return for further spiritual refreshment.

Right: Beinn Chabhair looking to Ben Cruachan (*David McLeod*)

BEINN A' CHROIN

3084ft/940m Mountain of harm or danger

As its name implies this hill is less than straightforward, and in mist careless use of map and compass may lead to awkward situations as everywhere its flanks are steep and rough with outcrops. Visitors need to look to each step on the complexities of a twisted and twinned summit, and the connecting ridges to hills on either hand.

Below: Beinn a' Chroin from the Cruach Ardrain-Beinn Tulaichean col (*Ruaridh Pringle*)

BEINN TULAICHEAN

3104ft/946m The knolly mountain

A true Brae of Balquhidder, alternatively known as hill of the hillocks, its various hummocks add attraction to a hill most often used as a stepping stone to its higher neighbour.

CRUACH ARDRAIN

3432ft/1046m The high heap

The term 'cruach' more usually signifies a stack, giving an alternative translation as 'stack of the high part'. Another hill popular with the early pioneers who relished the steep *couloir* of the Y Gully on its northern flank which, when filled with snow, gives a direct and exhilarating clamber to the summit cairn.

A favoured round is the circuit around Cruach Ardrain's northern corrie with a diversionary walk along a southern ridge to take in Beinn Tulaichean, the ease of the link much appreciated and anticipated when seen from Stob Garbh.

Right: Beinn Tulaichean and Cruach Ardrain from Stob Garbh (*Paul Craven*)

BEN MORE

3852ft/1174m Big mountain

Though not the highest mountain in Perthshire, the monarch of Glen Fillan is noted for its uncompromising steepness. One of the big days in the Scottish hills, more especially if continuing to the neighbouring Stob Binnein.

STOB BINNEIN

3822ft/1165m The pinnacle or anvil peak

The name is derived either from the Gaelic 'binnein' meaning peak, or 'innean' meaning anvil. Either would be appropriate as its flat anvil-head summit gives the mountain a particular distinction. Stob Binnein is lord of the Balquhidder hills and defers not to Ben More, and is its equal in all respects, the two being inseparable and a distinguished landmark for miles around.

One does not have to be a mountaineer to appreciate the grandeur of these giants as any motorist who has driven along Glen Dochart or Strath Fillan will testify.

Left: Ben More and Stob Binnein from Dalrigh (*Irvine Butterfield*)

BEN VORLICH

3231ft/985m Mountain of the bag-shaped bay

This mountain has similar features to the mountain of the same name above Loch Lomond and also has a dwelling called Ardvorlich at its foot suggesting like origins. Older spellings of Binvouirlyg and later Benvurlich may have indicated links with murlach, the kingfisher, but this is unlikely given the bird's preference for nesting sites beside sluggish streams. As the easier of two Loch Earn-side hills Ben Vorlich enjoys the greater popularity, especially in summer when ascent from Ardvorlich is enlivened with colourful flowers such as the foxglove.

Above: Ben Vorlich from Glen Vorlich (*Irvine Butterfield*)

STUC A' CHROIN

3199ft/975m Peak of harm or danger

A memorial plaque on the cairn of a northern top is a salutary reminder of the danger which gave this hill its title. Its buttress of crags looks more formidable a proposition under snow and may give its aspirant conquerors pause for thought on descent to the col linking the hill to its neighbour.

Left: Stuc a' Chroin from Bealach an Dubh Choirein (*John Digney*)

BEN CHONZIE

3054ft/931m The mountain of weeping

Ben y Hone, or Beinn Chaoineidh, are the alternative names for this bland hill. The latter name, the hill of weeping, is said to be derived from the Caledonians defeated by the Romans at Comrie, who buried their dead in Glen Turret, the glen of burial. The hill's ease of approach by the track from Glen Lednock lacks the interest of the walk into the bosom of the hills beside Loch Turret with the return across the outlying tops on the way to the convenient car-park at the Turret dam.

Right: Ben Chonzie and Loch Turret (*Irvine Butterfield*)

SCHIEHALLION

3553ft/1083m Fairy hill of the Caledonians
Whether you believe in fairies or not this
hill is an enchanting view-point with
undisputed claim to lie at the heart of
Scotland, hence the patriotic toast of the
Rannoch highlanders 'Here's to the back
o' Schiehallion'.

Pictures of Schiehallion usually
feature Loch Tummel or Loch Rannoch
but whatever the view-point water always
pays the finest compliment to this most
popular hill.
Right: Schiehallion and Dunalastair
Water from Drumglas (*Irvine Butterfield*)

CARN MAIRG

3418ft/1042m Hill of sorrow or of the dead
As the greatest of the Glen Lyon heights
its name is said to derive from Carn na
Marbh, and commemorates the Gatar
Mor, or Great Plague, finally turned back
near Slatich by St Eonan. Of the residents
of Fortingall only an old lady and a white
horse survived, and bore the responsibility
for burying the villagers. They are said to
lie in a mound marked by a cairn, the
cairn of the dead, in the field in front of
the hotel.

As the highest mountain in its group
the attainment of the cairn is often quite
literally the high point on the round
above Invervar.

Left: To the Ben Lawers group from Carn
Mairg (*Mike Dales*)

STUCHD AN LOCHAIN

3149ft/960m Peak of the little loch

This hill boasts one of the first recorded ascents of any Scottish hill. In the 1590s the dispossessed chief of the Campbells of Glen Lyon, Cailean Gorach, or Mad Colin, attended by his servant Findlay, came upon a herd of wild goats on the summit. Frustrated by a day of ill fortune at the hunt, Mad Colin drove the goats over the cliff into the corrie of Lochan nan Cat, and ordered his servant to leap after them. The loyal Findlay asked for a moment to say a prayer. While on his knees he noticed that Colin had wandered to the edge of the precipice. Seizing his chance, the quick-witted servant leaped upon his master, releasing him only on promise of Colin's future good behaviour.

On a clear day when views extend across the great waste of Rannoch Moor to Buachaille Etive Mor, distant sentinel of Glen Coe, 'The Stuic' is the place to be.
Right: Stuchd an Lochain looking to Buachaille Etive Mor (*Tom Rix*)

CREAG MHOR, OR MEALL NAN AIGHEAN

3218ft/981m Big rock, or hill of the heifers or hinds

Curiously this peak bears no name and has until recently been identified as Creag Mhor, a lower cragged height to the east. Other rocks break up the face above Glen Lyon to which the hill owes its allegiance. The later appellation is equally apt as there are ruined shielings in the high corrie to the east where summer grazing for cattle might be had, and where today deer graze. In mist its crown can confuse as it possesses two cairns of almost equal height some distance apart.

CARN GORM

3376ft/1029m Blue hill

Any hint of blue is associated with the dark hues of the grasses for these were there long before the dark pines crept up the lower slopes.

These two peaks represent the outward points of a horseshoe ridge above the tiny settlement of Invervar in Glen Lyon and as such look to each other across the broad sweep of Coire a' Chearcaill.

Above: Carn Gorm from the west top of Meall nan Aighean (*Irvine Butterfield*)

MEALL GARBH

3176ft/968m Rough rounded hill

A bald summit of stones little more than a high point on a rambling ridge provides the clue to a name which is descriptive rather than inspirational. If the visitors to its cairn remember it at all, imaginations are stretched to recount their day.

Recourse to the weather as a talking point seems to be a recurrent theme and clearly this hill has an image problem.
Above: Meall a' Bharr looking to Meall Garbh (*David McLeod*)

MEALL BUIDHE

3054ft/931m Rounded yellow hill

Yellowed grasses account for the name
and though most frequently climbed from
Loch an Daimh on the Glen Lyon side,
the hill really belongs to Rannoch as its
long fingers dip to the shores of that loch.

When the tawny grasses of summer
appear they illustrate why the hill took its
name from a predominant colour to
differentiate it from similarly rounded
hills close by. This is the highest of a
range of broad backed hills and its ascent
can be made without undue exertion –
one for a lazy day.

Below: The summit ridge from the south-
east top, Meall Buidhe (*Irvine Butterfield*)

BEN LAWERS

*3983ft/1214ft Speaking hill or hill of
clamour*

In the summer of 1878 one Malcolm
Ferguson engaged thirty men and two
masons to build a 20ft-high cairn. Nature
has since eroded this futile obelisk which
was to have placed the mountain's highest
point in the select band of 4000ft peaks.
The loud noise of the masons' hammering
does not account for the name which
predates this frenzied activity and is said
to relate to the tumult of the mountain's
many draining streams.

BEINN GHLAS

3619ft/1103m Greenish-grey mountain

Smoothed grassed slopes account for the
colouration and hence the simple and
unpretentious name.

Ease of winter access made this one
of the first venues for winter downhill ski-
ing, and the traverse of these hills is a
popular winter circuit for the
mountaineer.

Right: Ben Lawers and Beinn Ghlas from
An Stuc (*John Allen*)

AN STUC

3668ft/1118m The steep rock or the peak

The name of this mountain may appear incongruous as the traverse of its ridge is for the most part grass but the very steepness of its eastern edge urges caution, especially if wet or frosted.

Although the oblique view from Ben Lawers hides the steeper section, discerning mountaineers will note the craggy face and decline of the ridge beyond.

Left: An Stuc from Ben Lawers (*Tom Rix*)

MEALL GREIGH

3284ft/1001m Hill of horse studs

At one time horses were pastured on the hill's lower slopes around the Lawers Burn and the provision of grazing for them suggests easy slopes. A path provides an easy stair to the upper hill so that this approach is that most favoured to reach the lower slopes and gain this height by the lazy drift of the slopes above the stream's source in Lochan nan Cat.

Left: Meall Greigh and Lochan nan Cat from Creag an Fhithich (*Irvine Butterfield*)

MEALL GARBH

3668ft/1118m Rough round hill

Like several of the mountains which bear this name the hill has some minor crags which ruffle its upper slope immediately below the cairn.

The rocky ornaments and broken ground add to the interest of this otherwise unremarkable hill. All are easily by-passed on traverses to or from An Stuc.

Above: Meall Garbh from An Stuc (*Mike Dales*)

MEALL CORRANAICH

3507ft/1069m Round hill of the corrie of bracken

Another hill with the origins of its name lost in the mists of time. There may be bracken a-plenty but its name may also be variously interpreted as notched, prickly, hooked or crooked hill. It is also known as the hill of lamenting, or weeping of the type associated with funerals. This suggests a connection with the transport of the dead across the hill to the burial grounds in the neighbouring glens. The Munroist has little to lament as its ascent is easily accomplished from the hill crossing of Lochan na Lairige.

Left: Meall Corranaich from Meall nan Tarmachan (*John Allen*)

MEALL A' CHOIRE LEITH

3038ft/926m Round hill of the grey corrie

The grey corrie lies on an eastern slope, its scree spills the one hint of ruggedness on an otherwise unremarkable hill. Only from the higher ground to the east is there any appreciation of the hill's character as from most other directions it is either hidden or appears as an extended ridge of its near neighbour.

Right: Meall a' Choire Leith from Meall Garbh (*Irvine Butterfield*)

MEALL GHAORDAIDH

3409ft/1039m Round hill of the wrist

Hill of the shoulder, arm or hand, from the Gaelic 'gairdean' it may be to some but to the older inhabitants of Glen Lyon it was the round hill of the wrist. Whatever the choice, the mountain extends knuckles of crag towards the northern glen and a welcoming hand to all who climb it from that quarter.

Buttressing crags on this northern flank shadow the small farm at Moar in stark contrast to the bland slopes above the southern approaches from Glen Lochay.

Left: Meall Ghaordaidh from Gallin (*Irvine Butterfield*)

MEALL NAN TARMACHAN

3422ft/1043m Round hill of the ptarmigan

The ptarmigan are likely to get little peace for the hill's many visitors obviously enjoy the knolly ridge out to Creag na Caillich, with the uneasy crossing of a narrow *aréte* to the west of Meall Garbh adding to the enjoyment of the circuit.

The main summit of the mountain is rather bland and its views are left to rectify the loss of attraction on that account and to entice walkers along the ridge towards the first distinctive knot.

Below: Meall Garbh and Beinn nan Eachan from Meall nan Tarmachan (*John Allen*)

BEINN HEASGARNICH

3530ft/1076m Sheltering, peaceful mountain

This hill is one which appears on some of the earliest maps sometimes with a letter 's' before the 'h' in the form of sheasgarnich suggesting the name is one of ancient origin, as the letter 'h' stands before words beginning with a vowel and is not otherwise acknowledged in the Gaelic alphabet. Possibly from 'seasgair', sheltered or comfortable, as the value of its sheltering bulwark would be well recognised by those who tended their cattle at the shielings in its eastern hollows. The hill seen from afar appears as a long, almost level ridge which once gained affords extensive views.

CREAG MHOR

3435ft/1047m Big rock

Large rocky buttresses flank a summit set at a junction of ridges. In all probability these account for the chosen name, as they would appear to impede access to the crest.

The great back of Beinn Heasgarnich curves westwards to a boggy hill pass, Bealach na Bainteaghearna, beyond which rise the blunt walls of Creag Mhor. On a linked traverse these are outflanked by a detour to the low point of a northern spur to provide the easiest access to the cairn.

Right: Creag Mhor from Beinn Heasgarnich (*John Allen*)

SGIATH CHUIL

3015ft/919m Back wing

The back wing which gives the hill its name is a fine nebbed point on the southern end of its ridge, which, if the back of the mountain, suggests that those who named it lived in Glen Lochay to the north. It has also been known as Sgiath Chrom, crooked wing, and named as such by the Reverend A.R.G. Burn in his diary of Munro ascents. The escarped end to which the hill owes its title is most easily identified by the west-bound traveller heading along Strath Fillan.

Below: Sgiath Chuil from Luib (*Irvine Butterfield*)

BEINN DORAIN

3530ft/1076m Mountain of the streamlet

Another hill name of uncertain origin which may come from the Gaelic 'dobhran', an otter. Recent researches suggest 'the hill of the streamlet', many of which have seamed the steep slopes. On approaches from the south the mountain presents itself to the traveller as a perfect cone.

Above: Beinn Dorain from the south (*Irvine Butterfield*)

BEN CHALLUM

3363ft/1025m Malcolm's mountain

The older spelling of the name is 'Beinn Chaluim' which suggests a connection with St Columba, known to the Gaels as Colum Cille, Columba of the cell, and from which the surnames Malcolm and MacCallum are derived. There are other incidences of place names connected with the saint, and his biographer St Adamnan, in other localities in the Southern Highlands, so why not a mountain?

A long southern ridge to twin summits or by way of a ridge climbing from Glen Lochay are the most popular routes of ascent and are here seen from Meall Glas touched by mist and sun.

Above: Ben Challum from Meall Glas (*David May*)

MEALL GLAS

3140ft/957m Greenish-grey hill

With greater and more shapely hills around it is hardly surprising that this hill was simply named. The greenish-grey typifies a grassy hill and with the curvature of the hill providing a sheltered northern hollow it would be familiar to the inhabitants of Glen Lochay who probably named it.

Outcrops on the southern slopes below the summit must be negotiated on returns to Auchessan and provide added interest as well as a useful foil to distant views of mountains catching the last rays of a dying sun.

Right: Sunset from Meall Glas (*Irvine Butterfield*)

BEINN AN DOTHAIDH

3294ft/1004m Mountain of the scorching

Scorching in the sense that the south facing slopes would be a sun-trap. The summit on inspection is a table of stone-spattered grass possessing three high points, the central one holding most attraction for the Munroist. Those whose enjoyment demands that a decent view be had for their labours will direct their footsteps to the westerly hump. As if to thwart its visitors a combination of guardian crags, steep flanks and an irregular shape at the angle of ridges to adjacent peaks makes the hill an awkward neighbour. Views from either partner hint at the navigational difficulties.

Left: Beinn an Dothaidh from Beinn Achaladair (*Iain A. Robertson*)

BEINN MHANACH

3127ft/953m Monk's mountain

Long ago the route through the head of Glen Lyon was that used by the MacGregors carrying their dead to the clan burial ground in Glen Orchy. Travellers were ministered to by the monks of a small monastery at the foot of the hill, whose name is all that remains to record their vigil. Nowadays most of the traffic is in the opposite direction, many walkers seeking out this shy mountain by way of the path up the Auch Gleann.

Below: Beinn Mhanach from Auch Gleann (*John Digney*)

BEINN ACHALADAIR

3405ft/1038m Mountain of the field of hard water

The field of hard water is the area of ground subjected to winter's flood and frost which marks the overspill of the Water of Tulla in the flats at the foot of the mountain, close to the decaying ruins of the ancient stronghold of the Fletchers.

BEINN A' CHREACHAIN

3546ft/1081m Mountain of the plunderers

This peak stands guard above one of the ancient drove routes to and from Skye and in its time witnessed thousands of cattle on the move. Some of these were stolen by reiving bands from Lochaber who frequently plundered the cattle from the rich lands of the Campbells of Glen Lyon.

Beinn a' Chreachain is the most outlying of the Beinn Dorain group and is consequently often the last link in the chain of a traverse of all four peaks or is grouped with its near neighbour in a twosome traverse. It looks a 'tidy stretch' from Ben Dorain to Beinn a' Chreachain and it is!

Above: Beinn Achaladair and Beinn a' Chreachain from Beinn Dorain (*John Digney*)

THE CENTRAL HIGHLANDS

THE CENTRAL HIGHLANDS PROVIDED THE SETTING FOR THE SECOND MAJOR PHASE of Scottish mountaineering. The ridges and crags of Glen Coe provided inspiration to those proficient on rock, with the great ranges of Lochaber and the central Grampians to tempt those curious enough to expand their horizons. In the earliest years of exploration the railway was frequently used to gain access to a magnificent array of peaks in the heartland from points along the lines north to Inverness and west to Fort William.

Left: Buachaille Etive Mor from Altnafeadh (*Paul Craven*)

BEN CRUACHAN

3694ft/1126m Mountain of peaks or stacky hill

'Cruachan', war cry of the Campbells, strictly speaking applies to the whole ridge of peaks, the title having been usurped to give an identity to the highest point of all. In views from far and near the summit spire is unmistakable, a final horn adding to the visual effect of a superior height. This finishing touch also adds to the elation when gaining this spectacular belvedere of jumbled rock, more especially when approached by either the east or west ridges.

Left: Ben Cruachan from the west ridge (*Ruaridh Pringle*)

STOB DIAMH

3274ft/998m Peak of the stag

One of Cruachan's many tops which was the chosen Munro mountain representative of the heights of that great mountain's eastern ridges. When remnants of snow highlight gully and ridge it is excuse enough to be out and about on any of Cruachan's tops, a pleasure enhanced by the prospect of a crisp day as cloud curtains clear to reveal the engirdling peaks.

Right: The east ridge of Ben Cruachan looking to Stob Diamh (*Ruaridh Pringle*)

BEINN A' CHOCHUILL

3215ft/980m Mountain of the hood or shell

From most valley view-points this hill tends to be obscured behind its larger brethren but its summit gives expansive views along Loch Etive and across the shoulder of Cruachan to the Firth of Lorn.

BEINN EUNAICH

3245ft/989m Fowling mountain

The high point of a group of hills which form the boundary between Glen Strae and Glen Kinglass and like its twin, Beinn a' Chochuill, tends to be upstaged by the shapelier Ben Cruachan.

These hills are natural twins and whatever the route to the summits their combined circuit is one to relish views to Cruachan and the surrounding peaks.

Left: Beinn a' Chochuill from Beinn Eunaich (*David May*)

BEINN NAN AIGHENAN

3140ft/957m Mountain of the hinds

To the Munroist this hill is the odd one out on the round of high peaks ranged above Glen Etive. A point of decision is reached at the col east of Ben Starav. Many a Munroist has cause to agonise about a hill which may seem unattractive as it involves both a loss of height on the walk out to it and the return from its rugged heap to the main ridge.

Below: Beinn nan Aighenan from Stob Coire Dheirg (*Richard Wood*)

GLAS BHEINN MHOR

3271ft/997m Big greenish-grey mountain

The Gaels gave no great distinction to the hill when naming it and it would be easy to dismiss it as the linking summit between the castellated ridge of Ben Starav and the great bulk of its eastern neighbour. The discerning mountaineer will appreciate the beauty of a summit much enhanced by the bold face it presents to a northern corrie and the steep decline to an eastern divide.

Right: Glas Bheinn Mhor from Stob Coire Dheirg (*John Digney*)

BEN STARAV

3537ft/1078m Strong mountain

Strong in the sense that it is assertive, claiming the instant attention of travellers down Glen Etive. With a finely honed eastern ridge this is a firm favourite of the Munroist. Distance lends its own enchantment, the eastern ridge always the tell-tale feature to assist in the mountain's identification.

Above: Ben Starav across Lairig Eilde (*John Digney*)

STOB COIR' AN ALBANNAICH

3425ft/1044m Peak of the corrie of the Scots (the literal translation means 'the peak of the corrie of the men of Alba', the ancient Gaelic name for Scotland)

Local keepers refer to the hill as 'The Highlander' which confirms that its name dates from that time when the Scots who crossed from Ireland were newly settled in this part of the ancient kingdom of Dalriada.

To east and west it exposes great seamed flanks and the abiding memory of visitors to its cairn is the long drag to the summit.

Left: Stob Coir' an Albannaich from Meall nan Gobhar (*Irvine Butterfield*)

MEALL NAN EUN

3044ft/928m Hill of the birds

Another hill where a plenteous supply of grouse or other edible fowl was called into play to give identity to a peak often regarded as of little importance compared to its neighbours. This does the hill an injustice as it is uniformly steep with a north-west ridge the only straightforward route to its summit.

The mountain suffers from its proximity to higher and grander ridges close at hand, detaching itself with difficulty in a limited range of views from Glen Dochard.

Below: Meall nan Eun from Loch Dochard (*John Digney*)

STOB GHABHAR

3576ft/1090m Peak of the goats

One of the many peaks in Scotland where goats once roamed. They would certainly have clambered about the crags of the upper *couloir* which, with its renowned gully cleaving the headwall, offers superb sport under winter's ice and snow.

STOB A' CHOIRE ODHAIR

3100ft/945m Peak of the dun-coloured corrie

In the presence of Stob Ghabhar this peak may be of secondary interest but should not be so readily dismissed for it affords a fine panoramic view of the Moor of Rannoch and the Bridge of Orchy peaks.

A combined winter ascent is enlivened by their linking ridge, or if winter climbing attracts try the great *couloir* of Stob Ghabhar.

Right: Stob a' Choire Odhair and Stob Ghabhar from the path to Ba Bridge (*John Digney*)

CREISE

3609ft/1100m Grease or fat

The Gaelic 'creis', denotes grease or fat, and is a reference by the local Etive herdsmen to the quality of the grazing grounds which fattened their animals. Nowadays the translation may be given as narrow ridge. This high point only achieved prominence on metric mapping, taking precedence over Clach Leathad at the opposite end of the long ridge between Glen Etive and the Black Mount.

Left: Creise and Clach Leathad from Stob a' Ghlais Choire (*John Allen*)

MEALL A' BHUIRIDH

3635ft/1108m Hill of the bellowing

There are stags to be heard bellowing in the sanctuary of Coireach a' Ba where once John Scandoner, luckless servant of James VI and I, sought to capture an elusive white hind.

No matter the time or season, on a clear day the stone-studded lochans fringing Rannoch Moor provide the perfect foil to Meall a' Bhuiridh.

Right: Clach Leathad and Meall a' Bhuiridh from Lochan na h-Achlaise (*Ian Evans*)

BUACHAILLE ETIVE MOR – STOB DEARG

3353ft/1022m Big herdsman of Etive –
Red peak

Superlatives are the order of the day when attempting to describe 'The Buachaille' as it is affectionately known. Crags abound with classic climbs but there are less taxing ascents to its superb belvederes, of which Stob Dearg is the most popular.

There is much to interest cragsmen and hill-walker alike, the latter rejoicing that Stob Dearg is but one of a superb line of tops between the Glen Coe road and Glen Etive. Neighbouring Bidean nam Bian, seen as a complex of ridges, makes the climb to Stob Dearg well worth the effort.

Left: Bidean nam Bian from the summit of Stob Dearg (*Ian Evans*)

STOB COIRE RAINEACH

3035ft/925m Peak of the corrie of the ferns

This is another example of a high point being given a name already attached to the bracken corrie immediately below it which would be more familiar to those who took their stock to the hill and grazed the low ground about Loch na Fola.

Right: Stob Coire Raineach and Loch na Fola (*Ian Evans*)

STOB NA BROIGE

3136ft/956m Peak of the shoe

The name suggests that at a time when the highlander wore the rough hide shoe, or brogue, an incident occurred leading to the loss of such an item. This was thenceforth used by those native to the district as the means of identifying this particular peak.

STOB DUBH

3143ft/958m Black peak

The smaller of the Etive herdsmen does not have the craggy features of his brother peak but is the equal in all other respects, with steep flanks accentuating the spaciousness below a finely poised summit cairn.

The main summit of Buachaille Etive Beag, The Little Herdsman of Etive, and the Etive peak of the Big Herdsman sit as twin spires either side of the deep divide of Lairig Gartain and are a well-known study from Lochan Urr.

Right: Stob Dubh and Stob na Broige from Glen Etive (*Ian Evans*)

BIDEAN NAM BIAN

3773ft/1150m Pinnacle of the mountains

The highest point in the old county of Argyll, to the traveller through Glen Coe it is the sight of the buttressed 'Three Sisters', the ridges of Beinn Fhada, Gearr Aonach, and Aonach Dubh, that excites. A local minister, the Reverend Hugh Fraser, writing in the 'New Statistical Account' in the mid-nineteenth century, gave the name Ben-veedan, the 'peak of the deer skins'. This is often given by later writers as 'pinnacle of the hides'. Probably, and more correctly, it should be Bidean nam Beann, as it is certainly the culmination of a magnificent set of peaks. Given the right combination of rising mist and snow one might imagine it as truly Alpine.

Left: Bidean nam Bian massif from Am Bodach (*John Allen*)

STOB COIRE SGREAMHACH

3517ft/1072m Point of the dreadful corrie

The dreadful, or fearful, corrie which gave its name to this peak might refer to one of several which lie immediately below the mountain summit, for all routes to its cairn give airy views into rough hollows. Munroists now have greater excuse to visit its airy tower since it was elevated to mountain status on revision of *Munro's Tables*. The true mountaineer may scorn such titles for the onset of winter is encouragement enough to seek the high tops such as this.

Right: Looking south-west from Stob Coire Sgreamhach (*Jim Teesdale*)

SGORR NAM FIANNAIDH

3172ft/967m Peak of the Fianns

This is the one peak which celebrates the ancient race of the Fianna, a band of legendary folk heroes noted for their military and hunting prowess. Walkers may seek to emulate their ancestors with feats of daring on the narrow *arête* leading to the summit from the east – one of the classic traverses of the Scottish mountains.

Left: Aonach Eagach looking towards Sgorr nam Fiannaidh (*John Allen*)

SGOR NA H-ULAIDH

3261ft/994m Peak of the treasure

As the chieftain of the Glencoe MacDonalds resided at Gleann-leac-na-muidhe at the mountain's foot, treasure acquired by fair means or foul might find safe keeping in the hills. Today's treasures are the moments spent among the hills with this peak offering its own rewards.

Left: Sgor na h-Ulaidh from Beinn Maol Chaluim (*John Allen*)

MEALL DEARG

3127ft/953m Red hill

It is recorded that this peak was the last ascent of the first Munroist, the Reverend A.E. Robertson, who first kissed the cairn and then his accompanying wife. Since that time many have attained a summit whose modest title gives no hint of the exposure and difficult steps on either approaches to this eastern mountain of the famed Aonach Eagach. Despite the presence of a well-worn path, approaches to Meall Dearg are tricky for it is *de rigeur* to make the ridge traverse a part of one's ascent.

Above: Meall Dearg from Stob Coire Leith (*Tom Rix*)

SGORR DHONUILL

3284ft/1001m Donald's peak

As the mountain lies in the heartland of the Glen Coe MacDonalds the mountain may have been a favourite of the first chieftain of that clan.

The steep climb tops out around a cove of crags buttressing the rocky summit, a fine finale to the traverse of Beinn a' Bheithir with extensive views along the Firth of Lorn.

Below: Sgorr Dhonuill from Sgorr Dhearg (*John Allen*)

SGORR DHEARG

3359ft/1024m Red peak

Another mountain height with a name which merely indicates its hue as seen by those who named it. Mountaineers better recognise the gracious sweep of the ridge which guides them to the summit from the lower point of Sgorr Bhan.

Right: Sgorr Dhearg from Sgorr Bhan (*John Digney*)

BEINN SGULAIRD BEINN SGULAIRD

3074ft/937m Hill of the hat

The Gaelic 'sgulair' is a possible origin of this hill's name. Meaning 'an old hat', thisa is not an implausible description of the shape of the mountain when seen sideways on as it could be likened to a large crumpled hat with a dent in the crown.

A lengthy ridge comes with a recommendation to look seaward across the Firth of Lorn to the distant hills on Mull.

Above: Loch Creran and Mull from Beinn Sgulaird (*Jim Teesdale*)

BEINN A' BHEITHIR

Mountain of the monster

The monster was a serpent which devoured passers-by until Charles the Skipper tempted it with a sumptuous feast aboard his ship, only to be reached across a causeway of barrels filled with pointed stakes. In its haste to secure the food the impatient and greedy beast was fatally impaled on the spikes.

BINNEIN BEAG

3094ft/943m Small peak or pinnacle
Small in relation to its larger neighbour its distinct haycock shape refuses to be upstaged by its grander companion. There can be no doubt it seeks recognition to be claimed a mountain in its own right, and such it deserves to be.

BINNEIN MOR

3707ft/1130m Big peak or pinnacle
The highest peak of the Mamores and obviously big in every sense, a lord of the forest, easily recognised by the traveller on the road beside Loch Leven or by the back-packer on the path through Glen Nevis.

Viewed from the high ground above Glen Nevis a clear divide is seen between these two peaks so that both seem equally ennobled.

Right: Binnein Beag and Binnein Mor from Ben Nevis (*John Allen*)

SGURR EILDE MOR

3314ft/1010m Big peak of the hinds
The deer still graze the heights of this hill which, like many others, maintains its association with the chase.

As the eastern outlier of the Mamores the hill stands aloof, its summit battlement guarded by moating lochs and a rampart of screes.

Above: Sgurr Eilde Mor and Loch Eilde Mor (*David May*)

BEINN FIONNLAIDH

3146ft/959m Finlay's mountain
This hill is one of two so named. The other peak in the Affric hills was named after a gamekeeper in MacKenzie country. It is doubtful if at this remove that either the keeper, or knowledge of his temper, would be considered such as to merit the naming of a second hill in recognition of his legendary character. Most probably the name refers to someone who once hunted, or lived, in the locality.
Right: Beinn Fhionnlaidh from Fasnacloich (*Irvine Butterfield*)

NA GRUAGAICHEAN

3461ft/1055m The damsels

Another mountain which owes its name to Gaelic lore. Upon this hill-top a hunter met two damsels who gave to him a hunting dog which (like other mythical hounds) was the finest which ever lived. The mountain is easily identified by its twin summits, each a maiden in mountain form.

Left: Summit ridge Na Gruagaichean (*John Digney*)

AM BODACH

3386ft/1032m The old man

The term 'old man' as applied to a hill is not confined to Scotland, and was often commonly used to give character and identity to a prominent or distinguished hill above a settlement.

STOB COIRE A' CHAIRN

3218ft/981m Peak of the corrie of the cairn

The corrie of the cairn lies tucked under the summit at the head of a broader hollow where cattle were once pastured in the summer months. The cairns probably marked an ancient boundary or upper limit of the grazings.

Am Bodach and Stob Coire a' Chairn mark the central dog-leg twist in the Mamores ridge as illustrated in the view from An Gearanach.

Below: Am Bodach and Stob Coire a' Chairn from An Gearanach (*John Digney*)

AN GEARANACH

3222ft/982m The complainer
Any complaint by the
Munroist will focus upon
the narrowness of the ridge
which is the culmination of
a sharp ascent from Steall
Falls in Glen Nevis.

There has been some
doubt over the years as to
which point is the higher of
the two. Buckle to and
make them part of a circuit
above the Falls of Steall and
enjoy the retrospective
views to Nevis as your
reward.

Right: An Gearanach
from An Garbhanach
(*John Digney*)

SGURR A' MHAIM

3605ft/1099m Peak of the breast

Viewed from Glen Nevis the mountain certainly takes the shape of a great breast though the name might also be interpreted as 'peak of the pass' as it guards the entrance to the route into upper Glen Nevis. A steep uncompromising ascent leads directly to its cairn though it is *de rigeur* to tackle it by its Devil's Ridge, one of the most photographed *arêtes* in the Scottish mountains. No apologies are offered for repeating the exercise in visual temptation for here is a classic example of a hill's outlying tops offering more aesthetic stimulus than the parent peak.

Left: Devil's Ridge from Sgurr a' Mhaim (*John Allen*)

MULLACH NAN COIREAN

3081ft/939m Top of the corries

As its title suggests the twists in its spine and terminal spurs create no fewer than five corries lorded over by this bland height. As the terminal Munro at the western end of the Mamores ridge its vistas down the Firth of Lorn uplift the spirit with dreams of the hills of Ardgour.

Above: Meall a' Chaorainn from Mullach nan Coirean (*John Allen*)

STOB BAN

3277ft/999m Pale peak

The quartzite stones of the mountain's summit are often confused with a mantle of snow and there is added sparkle to its summit as it is buttressed by a great wall of crags above an eastern corrie. This eastern prospect provides the grandest spectacle with none so fine as on a clear winter's day.

Right: Stob Ban from Sgurr a' Mhaim (*John Allen*)

BEN NEVIS

4409ft/1344m Venomous or malicious mountain

The Owl of Strone, a Gaelic poet familiar with the district, wrote in the sixteenth century of a Beinn Nimneis, which suggests 'venomous' or 'wicked'. About a century later, Blaeu's map, based on the cartography of Pont, gives the name Bin Nevesh, a possible attempt at phonetic spelling. Its name might equally be derived from the Gaelic 'Beinn-neamh-bhathais' which freely translated means 'the mountain with its head in the clouds'. This might be more apt for Britain's highest mountain which enjoys few days completely free of mist.

In a word, Ben Nevis is so dominant that even from lesser heights to the south its great flank and rounded dome are ever pre-eminent.
Right: Ben Nevis and Lochan Lunn Da Bhra (*Ian Evans*)

CARN MOR DEARG

4002ft/1220m Big red hill

The name is descriptive of the red pinnacles and rock to be found on this mountain which also lays claim to the narrow *arête* which links it to its neighbour, Ben Nevis.

The abiding memory for those who ascend this peak from the Allt a' Mhuilinn is the triple-topped ridge which first tantalises with a distant glimpse of the ultimate summit.
Opposite: The ridge Carn Mor Dearg (*John Allen*)

AONACH MOR

4005ft/1221m Big ridge

It is easy to see how this mountain got its name for it is the ridge thrusting out towards the Lochy that first catches the eye and when viewed from the Great Glen appears as a great back. Its secretive corries and buttresses are revealed more fully to those who tread the summit.

Left: Aonach Mor from Aonach Beag (*Richard Wood*)

SGURR CHOINNICH MOR

3589ft/1094m The big mossy peak

For a hill described as mossy its summit is surprisingly pointed which adds to its aesthetic appeal, and it is much admired by those who reach the attendant height of Stob Coire Easain.

Below: Sgurr Choinnich Mor from Stob Coire Easain (*John Digney*)

AONACH BEAG

4048ft/1234m Little ridge

More dome than ridge, this mountain suffers from its proximity to Aonach Mor from which it is most easily approached.

On climbs from Glen Nevis by way of an eastern ridge one can enliven the interest by keeping to an edge peering into the crag-fast confines of a northern corrie.

Above: Aonach Beag across An Aghaidh Gharbh (*John Digney*)

STOB COIRE AN LAOIGH

3661ft/1116m Peak of the corrie of the calf (young deer)

The hill takes its name from the corrie on the Glen Nevis flank which does little to portray the mass of stone on its summit and the grey scree fans which give to the range the collective name 'Grey Corries'. This is the western summit of the main section of the ridge which extends across a series of lesser summits from Stob Choire Claurigh.

Left: Stob Coire an Laoigh and the ridge from Stob Choire Claurigh (*John Digney*)

STOB CHOIRE CLAURIGH

3861ft/1177m Peak of the brawling corrie

The several corries tucked under the ridges of this hill are the haunt of stags and this association undoubtedly gave the mountain its name. On a clear spring morning there is always the promise of one of those halcyon days long remembered so that even those looking from the low ground might be tempted to gaze and wonder.

Below: Stob Choire Claurigh from Bohuntine (*Irvine Butterfield*)

STOB BAN

3205ft/977m Pale peak

Although a part of the Grey Corries range, the bleached peak of Stob Ban is somewhat isolated from the main thrust of the ridge and its proud horn can be seen distantly from as far as Loch Laggan-side with its peak progressively intruding upon the skyline on approaches to Glen Spean.

Right: Stob Ban from Laggan dam (*David May*)

CHNO DEARG

3432ft/1046m Red nut

Early maps gave the Gaelic 'cnoc' so that the mountain's true name is red hill, the colour here signifying the abundant presence of heather. Less attractive than its partnering peak, it often becomes but a footnote to the round of Coire an Lochain, its attraction garnered from another entry in the Munroist's list of conquests. In soft winter's snow it commands respect as it can seem an arduous and pointless struggle up from the col.

Below: Chno Dearg across Coire an Lochain (*Ralph Storer*)

STOB COIRE SGRIODAIN

3212ft/979m Peak of the scree corrie

It may seem curious that the scree corrie which gave the hill its name is that above the Loch Treig shore rather than the tarned hollow to the east, around which the hill curves. But it should be remembered there were residents on that western quarter long before the coming of the dam which raised the height of the loch. From the summit way beyond the head of Loch Treig there are glimpses of the peaks around the entrance to Glencoe.

Right: Buachaille Etive Mor from Stob Coire Sgriodain (*Irvine Butterfield*)

STOB A' CHOIRE MHEADHOIN

3625ft/1105m Peak of the middle corrie

The mountain takes its name from the middle of three steep-walled hollows whose streams tumble into Loch Treig. Travellers on the Glen Spean road see this as a conical peak with its twin peering over a western shoulder.

STOB COIRE EASAIN

3658ft/1115m Peak of the corrie of the little cascade

The cascades of the streams which debouch into Loch Treig lie above an inhospitable shore seldom, if ever, visited by the rambler. Only its association with them gives credit to a mountain too frequently regarded as an adjunct to its twin.

These two peaks stand in splendid isolation which is no better demonstrated when temperature inversion sees them stand island-like tall above a sea of cloud.

Above: Stob a' Choire Mheadhoin and Stob Coire Easain from Creag Meagaidh (*Richard Wood*)

BEINN NA LAP

3074ft/937m Mottled mountain

To the Gael the mottled effect is intended to denote a defective spot in the colouration which, given the mixture of stone, grass and heather, seems apt.

Possessing no feature of real note this might be much neglected were it not a Munro. It is easily ascended from Corrour by the broad flank above Loch Ossian to which it pays court.

Left: Beinn na Lap looking to Corrour (*David May*)

CARN DEARG

3087ft/941m Red cairn

A ubiquitous mountain name, and like its kin red with heather. A modest and retiring hill, bounding the great waste of the Moor of Rannoch.

Along its foot runs the 'Road to the Isles' which meets the newer iron road of the West Highland Railway at Corrour, the highest point on the line.

Below: Carn Dearg from Corrour Summit (*Irvine Butterfield*)

SGOR GAIBHRE

3133ft/955m Peak of the goats

A one-time proliferation of goats hereabouts was recorded for posterity in the name given to this grassy knot. Its ascent is usually twinned with that of Carn Dearg which similarly thrusts out a lengthy spur, Sron Leachd a' Chaorainn, to ease access from the road to Rannoch's lonely station.

Above: Sgor Gaibhre from Sron Leachd a' Chaorainn (*Tom Rix*)

AONACH BEAG

3661ft/1116m Little ridge

A shapely hump, whose ascent is followed by a comparable descent, gives to this peak the appearance of a milestone on a lengthy ridge between the lochs of Ossian and Pattack.

GEAL-CHARN

3714ft/1132m White hill

The summit of this hill is surprisingly broad and totally bland considering the approaches to it, that of the Lancet Edge being a particularly fine and airy traverse above the Bealach Dubh.

The two mountains are linked and lie central to a range stretching from Loch Pattack to Loch Ossian in the remote heart of the Ben Alder Forest.

Left: Aonach Beag and Geal-Charn from the summit cairn of Beinn Eibhinn (*Richard Wood*)

BEINN EIBHINN

3615ft/1102m Delightful mountain

Sometimes translated as the mountain of the fair outlook, a not unworthy name given the view down Loch Ossian. Eibhinn or Aoibhinn, meaning delightful, would also be the Gaelic spelling for Aibind, one of the holy maidens subject to St Brigit. The church at Inch in Badenoch is supposed to have been dedicated to her, and though unrecorded it is just possible that she might have passed through the hills on her way from the west.

The fair outlook is almost certainly that down Loch Ossian to the hills fringing the Moor of Rannoch.

Left: Loch Ossian from Beinn Eibhinn (*Richard Wood*)

CARN DEARG

3392ft/1034m Red cairn

Not usually regarded a notable height, as from most directions it appears little more than the high point of a ridge flanked by steep heather terraces. With russet rock and heather for redness there is a choice – take your pick!

Those who take the long approach along the River Pattack find that from the bridge on the estate march the mountain appears at its most stately, especially when dressed in winter's ermine.

Right: Carn Dearg from River Pattack (*Irvine Butterfield*)

BEINN A' CHLACHAIR

3566ft/1087m Mountain of the stonemason

Whether the stonemasons who gave the hill its name found employment in the old clachans at the mountain's foot goes unrecorded, though they would have found ample material for their constructions on its crown and corrie.

As with most mountains the proximity of water adds to a mountain scene and on a clear winter's day there can be few more entrancing moments than such experiences in the heart of the hills.

Left: Beinn a' Chlachair from Loch Pattack (*Irvine Butterfield*)

CREAG PITRIDH

3031ft/924m Petrie's crag

Crags and hollows abound so it is possible that the origins of the mountain's name might lie in a similar mix of the Gaelic creag, 'a crag', and the Pictish pit, 'a hollow'. This would be unusual as most localities with 'pit' in the name refer to settlements. It is more likely named after one Petrie, who may have been employed locally as a keeper or shepherd, and this is the preferred choice.

From the most convenient view-points along the Laggan road the peak does not detach itself sufficiently from the parent Geal Charn, appearing at best as a small knot of crag. Closer inspection reveals bands of rock terraces lapped by the waters of the southern half of twin lochans.

Below: Creag Pitridh from Allt Meall Ardruighe Reservoir (*Jim Teesdale*)

GEAL CHARN – MULLACH COIRE AN IUBHAIR

3441ft/1049m White hill or top of the corrie of the yew tree

There are too many Geal Charns and with a prominent hollow separating its twin peaks 'the top of the corrie of the yew tree' is much the better name for so distinguished a peak. In bygone days many took the track by Loch Ericht and Loch Pattack to the old bothy beside the black burn, like the yew trees, alas, now gone.

Right: Geal Charn from Pattack track (*Irvine Butterfield*)

A'MHARCONAICH

3199ft/975m The horse place

In times past horses roamed the hills and as they were important to the economy, places where they gathered would be noted; it is probable than the slopes of this hill were such a place.

GEAL-CHARN

3008ft/917m White hill

The attainment of its cairn often marks the start or finish of the round of the four Munros west of Drumochter, and might be summarily dismissed on that account.

To travellers heading north on the Inverness road the blunt end of A'Mharconaich heralds the climb to the summit of Drumochter, and the passing of Balsporran cottages at the foot of Geal-charn confirms descent towards Badenoch.

Below: A'Mharconaich and Geal-charn from Carn na Caim (*Jim Maison*)

SGAIRNEACH MHOR

3251ft/991m Big rocky hillside

The rockiest slope is that of the north-facing Coire Creagach which adds shape and lustre to a hill set among others of lesser character.

BEINN UDLAMAIN

3317ft/1011m Mountain of the unsteady place

Gloomy is the other interpretation given to the Gaelic name of this great back. The great rocks scattered about a large summit cairn are a trap for unwary feet and the hill seems to attract more than its fair share of mist so that either interpretation will find its adherents.

There are many who take advantage of the easy access from the summit of Drumochter to speed ascents of the Munros ranged to the west of the pass, for here a gate marks the start of a welcome track through the drumlins in the foot of Coire Dhomhain.

Right: Sgairneach Mhor and Beinn Udlamain from Drumochter (*Irvine Butterfield*)

BEN ALDER

3766ft/1148m Mountain of rock water

As a mountain plateau which boasts a tarn said to be the highest in the Highlands, and with a grand cirque of crags, the mountain is synonymous with a derivation from the Gaelic 'alldhobhar', 'all' being a rock or precipice, and 'dhobhar' signifying water. The mountain has long been documented and was shown as Bin Aildir on the seventeenth-century maps of the famous Blaeu, and later in a Maclagan manuscript of 1755 the name is given as Beinn Eallair.

BEINN BHEOIL

3343ft/1019m The mountain in front

Most hill-goers have long understood Beinn Bheoil to mean the mountain in front of Ben Alder. Recent interpretation suggests 'the hill of the mouth' which might well refer to its situation above the mouth of the Alder Burn.

One does not need to be a walker to appreciate the magnificence of these mountains as the long trench of Loch Ericht parts the mountains to reveal a clear prospect of both Ben Alder's cliff and its shielding peak. Distance hints at their romantic remoteness and mystic allure.

Right: Ben Alder and Beinn Bheoil along Loch Ericht from Dalwhinnie (*Irvine Butterfield*)

BEINN A' CHAORAINN

3445ft/1050m Mountain of the rowan tree

Mapping of its triple tops has seen a change to the true summit, vexatious to the hill's gazetteers and those incautious enough to follow blindly the compass on misty winter days, oblivious to a corniced corrie edge. It is this edge which gives the hill character for otherwise its long whaleback ridge would excite little interest.

Left: Beinn a' Chaorainn centre top looking to the south top (*David McLeod*)

CREAG MEAGAIDH

3707ft/1130m Bogland rock

Those who once herded their cattle along the upper reaches of the Spey would have much wet ground to contend with, and looking to the inner recesses of the great range to the south would know of its crags and corries. The summit possesses two cairns, the largest of which is reputed to be the work of a madman built as a tribute to his wife.

It is not the bland summit of Creag Meagaidh which grabs the attention but its cliffs when plastered in snow. This is the domain of the ice-climber.

Right: Cliffs of Coire Ardair, Creag Meagaidh (*John Digney*)

BEINN TEALLACH

3002ft/915m Forge mountain

The vagaries of mapping meant that this mountain was a late entry to the Munro lists. Its name is a curiosity as there is no history to indicate the presence of a smithy, or forge, in the locality. The best explanation offered is that the shape of an eastern corrie resembles a hearth, though quite why this should be singled out remains a mystery.

Beinn Teallach also teases with its twin summit cairns which both appear to be of equal elevation, and sit either side of a shallow hollow parallel to and west of the main back of the ridge.

Below: Beinn Teallach looking south-west (*Jim Teesdale*)

CARN LIATH

3300ft/1006m Grey hill

The colour of the rocks dictates the name and walkers should not be surprised to encounter scree beds which beard its slopes and dapple its ridge.

Seen from the usual approach from the Laggan road as one of the summits on the northern bounds of Coire Ardair, Carn Liath lacks presence. That the mountain is seldom approached from the ancient route of the Corrieyairack to the north might be considered to its detriment as from this side the mountain presents a bolder front inviting exploration.

Right: Carn Liath from Melgarve (*Tom Rix*)

STOB POITE COIRE ARDAIR

3455ft/1053m Peak of the pot of the high corrie

This point lies above 'the window', a gap which separates the hill from Creag Meagaidh and by local tradition the route taken by Bonnie Prince Charlie on his journey from Achnacarry to meet Cluny MacPherson in his 'cage' on Ben Alder.

The cairn lies close to a cragged edge and is a fine belvedere from which to survey the great buttresses of Creag Meagaidh's cliffs.

Above: Cliffs of Coire Ardair from Stob Poite Coire Ardair (*David May*)

GEAL CHARN

3038ft/926m White hill

One of a profusion of such named hills in the district which suggests a rather unimaginative populace, who might have used the presence of a distinctive window in the ridge below the summit the better to identify the hill.

Left: Geal Charn from Glen Markie (*Irvine Butterfield*)

CARN SGULAIN

3018ft/920m Hill of the basket

For such a featureless hill it seems difficult to equate its shape with that of a bucket or basket, upturned or otherwise. Of all the Monadhliath Munros it is the most shapeless and uninteresting, an epithet as often applied to the range as to this single hill.

A'CHAILLEACH

3051ft/930m The old woman

The summit cairn sitting at the edge of an eastern scarp helps identify this hill, which may be one commemorating the legendary Cailleach Bheur who wandered the hills and summoned the deer hinds to milking with a siren-like voice. There are still hinds on the hills hereabouts but the

siren song is more likely to be that of the northerly winds which sweep the plateau.

The approach to A'Chailleach is made easier by a track along the Allt a' Chaorainn, but walkers must go beyond the stream crossing to catch sight of Carn Sgulain, a dull mound even by Monadhliath standards.

Left: A'Chailleach and Carn Sgulain from Allt a' Chaorainn (*Irvine Butterfield*)

CARN DEARG

3100ft/945m Red hill

The red may refer to rock or heather as the ridge can be very green in summer. The plateau across to the other heights takes on a new dimension when winter's hardened snows help make light work of the traverse.

Above: Plateau Carn Ban-Carn Dearg from Carn Ballach (*Irvine Butterfield*)

THE CAIRNGORMS

THE CAIRNGORMS ARE UNIQUE IN THAT THE VAST PLATEAU OF THE CENTRAL core of peaks still retains its arctic character where scant vegetation clings to an overburden of scanty soils and grits. Buttressing these bare uplands, magnificent corrie headwalls cosset the birthplace of streams. In so vast an area the glens which reach into the interior provide lines of approach. Access to the remoter corries, crags and cairns is thus the preserve of those prepared for the long walk in.

Left: Scorrie of Driesh from Glen Doll (*Paul Craven*)

MEALL CHUAICH

3120ft/951m Cup lump

The cup here is a quaich and the hill is said to derive its name from its shape, that of an upturned cup, or drinking vessel, or possibly takes its name from Loch Cuaich which sits in a bowl at its foot.

A line of poles beside a wide track and aqueduct evidence the hand of men who harnessed the waters of the Allt Cuaich. These intrusive artefacts spoil the wild quality and the hill suffers accordingly – for many it has become a hill merely to be bagged in the passing.

Left: Meall Chuaich from the Allt Cuaich (*Irvine Butterfield*)

CARN NA CAIM

3087ft/941m Cairn of the twist

The level summit of this hill sits at a curve in the ridge though the hill name might also be linked with that of the Cama Choire, or crooked corrie, secreted in its eastern folds.

A'BHUIDHEANACH BHEAG

3071ft/936m Little yellow place

The coarse yellow grasses of this rambling

hill add colour to an otherwise dull plateau and would seem to suggest the origin of its name.

These hills are cast in the same mould and such charm as they possess lies in the glorious feeling of space when tramping the plateau between the two, suggested in views from adjacent hills.

Above: Carn na Caim and A'Bhuidheanach Bheag from A'Mharconaich (*Irvine Butterfield*)

CARN AN FHIDHLEIR

3261ft/994m Hill of the fiddler

There is another hill to the north associated with a fiddler, but who he was is unrecorded. Perhaps he occupied a shieling in the upper reaches of the Feshie or was a travelling musician for there is a pass of the fiddler through the hills hereabouts. Now only the music of the wind drifts upon the air.

A curious tale attaches to this hill concerning Sir Hugh Munro. He climbed under cover of darkness to avoid interference with the stalking, and failed to locate the cairn. Therefore it remains one of the three summits which he did not claim. Search for a suitable photograph of the mountain met with similar failure and was only secured with difficulty.

Right: Carn an Fhidhleir from the River Feshie (*Martin Moar*)

BEINN DEARG

3307ft/1008m Red mountain

The presence of Druim Dubh, or black ridge, suggests that the heather is black rather than red thus dispelling that source of origin of the mountain's name. This is taken from the reddish granite boulders which break through the heathery coverlet of the summit ridge. These factors may seem of small account as the one abiding memory of this hill's ascent will be the lengthy walk in and the feeling of splendid isolation.

A mantle of snow further accentuates this aura of loneliness with the mountain seeming ever more distant, a forlorn and forgotten sentinel of the moors.

Below: Beinn Dearg and Beinn a' Chait from Meall Dubh (*Irvine Butterfield*)

CARN A' CHLAMAIN

3159ft/963m Hill of the kite or buzzard

The kite has long since disappeared and any buzzards which remain will have inherited a domain most easily reached on climbs from the Tilt to the summit.

As part of a vast spread of rolling heights the hill's individuality is best appreciated from a distance, a coverlet of snow restoring the majesty of a hill much scarred by a prominent track ascending the steep spur rising from the deep trench of Glen Tilt.

Right: Carn a' Chlamain from Kirkton of Lude (*Irvine Butterfield*)

AN SGARSOCH

3300ft/1006m Place of the sharp rocks

The name is thought to derive from An Sgarsach, a derivation of 'sgar', a knot or fissure. It was once known as An Sgarsach Mhor, there still being a smaller outlier to the north known as Scarsoch Bheag. Strange to think that on this hill there once was an annual cattle market, Feill Sgarsaich. Some of the sharp rocks have been gathered to construct a substantial cairn to mark its rather indifferent summit.

Whatever route is chosen to reach its lonely cairn, walkers are faced with long treks into the mountains, following one tributary or another of one of Scotland's great rivers as the hill lies on a watershed which sits above burns eager to join the Tay, Dee or Spey.

Above: An Sgarsoch from Feith Uaine Mhor (*Irvine Butterfield*)

BEINN A' GHLO

Mountain of the mist or veil

Beinn a' Ghlo is well named for it is one of those mountain ranges which attracts more than its fair share of mist which frequently hangs across the ridges and drapes the upper slopes. To the imaginative this effect suggests a veil, and when seen is very apt.

CARN LIATH

3199ft/975m Grey hill

Of all Beinn a' Ghlo's three mountain summits this is the most prominent and when seen from Killiecrankie and other view-points on the main road north appears as a conical hill with grey screes much in evidence. Attractive though this view may be it is marred by the scar of a path which claws its way directly to the summit.

BRAIGH COIRE CHRUINN-BHALGAIN

3510ft/1070m Upland of the corrie of the round blisters

Beinn a' Ghlo has no fewer than nineteen corries and legend has it that a rifle discharged in one cannot be heard in any of the others. The corrie which gave this central height its name lies to the south-west and is one of the feeders of the Fender Burn, a tributary of the Tilt.

CARN NAN GABHAR

3678ft/1121m Hill of the goats

The crown of the mountain was once populated by goats but these have long since disappeared. Those careless of the map may mistake the Ordnance Survey pillar for the summit which lies at a cairn a few yards further to the north-east.

Left: Beinn a' Ghlo from Ben Vrackie
(*Irvine Butterfield*)

CARN AN RIGH

3376ft/1029m Hill of the king

Malcolm II (1058–93) hunted here and must have created an impression on his subjects who were moved to give this hill a regal name. Less pretentious may be an origin in the word 'ruighe', or shieling, though the royal association does seem well established.

One of the more inaccessible peaks, its visitors are few, and from most directions it does not stand out as detached from mountains round about; the view from Carn Bhac probably gives as fine an appreciation of its station as any.

Left: Carn an Righ from Carn Bhac
(*Irvine Butterfield*)

GLAS TULAICHEAN

3448ft/1051m Green hillocks

The name speaks of green grasses and mark this out as an easy ascent. A fine eastern corrie gives character to a hill which in all other respects is a long rolling ridge. Ascents by way of Gleann Taitneachan to the east favour access to this corrie. A headwall decked in the last lingering snows of spring shows this facet of the mountain to advantage and adds interest on a clamber to the east ridge.

Above: Glas Tulaichean from Glas Choire Mhor (*Don Green*)

AN SOCACH (WEST SUMMIT)

3097ft/944m The snout

A snout in the sense that it is a projecting place. The prominence of the nose which pushes out towards Glen Ey suggests a name given by the long-forgotten inhabitants of that glen. Linked by a broad almost level ridge the two tops of this mountain have both had summit status. That farthest from the road in Glen Clunie now has title to the summit, thus providing an excuse to extend a fine day's excursion with rare glimpses of the hidden corners around the head of Glen Ey.

Below: Glas Tulaichean from An Socach (*Don Green*)

BEINN IUTHARN MHOR

3428ft/1045m Big hill of the edge-point

Big hell's peak, or hellish big hill, is often the interpretation of the name given though quite what this peak has about it to merit so terrible a fate as to be linked with the domain of the Prince of Darkness remains unexplained. More credible is a translation from the Gaelic 'Beinn Fhiubharainn Mhor', meaning a sharp-edge big hill. This is well illustrated in the spring when a snow wreath lingers along a finely honed northern edge.

Right: Summit ridge Beinn Iutharn Mhor (*David May*)

CARN BHAC

3104ft/946m Hill of the peat banks

The name may be a corruption of 'Carn Vaich' which suggests sheltering hill. The presence of peat banks at a higher altitude than usual is equally apt and this translation better prepares visitors for the squelchy peat encountered on this hill's flanks.

Perceptive study of the map shows that from the summit cairn there may be the possibility of a superb panorama of the major Cairngorm peaks – weather permitting!

Above: Beinn Bhrotain and The Devil's Point from Carn Bhac (*Irvine Butterfield*)

CARN AOSDA

3008ft/917m Hill of age

More properly Carn Aoise, hill of old age, suggesting antiquity. Quite why this particular hill should be so singled out for such recognition as one of great age remains unexplained. Certainly the ease of ascent commends it as a view-point reached with little effort so that the elders of the mountaineering fraternity may yet enjoy a magnificent vista of the Cairngorms. Skiers have done much to scar its slopes and though never regarded as an attractive hill it deserves better. The most inviting ascent lies from Glen Clunie to which the mountain presents a more pleasant face.

Left: Carn Aosda from Glen Clunie (*Irvine Butterfield*)

THE CAIRNWELL

3061ft/933m Hill of blisters or bags

Those who wonder how such a name could be arrived at must refer to the original Gaelic An Carn Bhalg, hill of the bags, which also has its counterpart in the adjacent Carn nan Sac, hill of the sack. Both refer to the pouches of peat banks on the lower slopes. Man's handiwork is much in evidence on the northern slopes so that the hill presents its fairest face to the south and the scoop of the Allt a' Choire Dhiridh.

Above: The Cairnwell across Allt a' Choire Dhiridh (*Irvine Butterfield*)

CARN A' GHEOIDH

3199ft/975m Hill of the goose

This seems a strange place to be associated with geese unless nesting on Loch Vrotachan to the north where they might have been a source of food in times long past. The hill itself is unpretentious, scarcely a ripple on a broad-backed ridge more often than not seen in silhouette from other mountain sanctuaries close by.

Right: Carn a' Gheoidh from The Cairnwell (*Tom Rix*)

CAIRN OF CLAISE

3491ft/1064m Hill of the hollow

Another name for the hill is said to be the green grassy place from the Gaelic Carn na Glaiseath but the Gaelic 'clais', a trench or pit, would be equally significant given the proximity of the attractive depths of Corrie Kander whose crags buttress the hill's northern slope.

CARN AN TUIRC

3343ft/1019m Hill of the boar

Wild boar once roamed the Highlands and here was obviously a hill of some interest to the legendary Fingalian hunters long before others hunted the animals to extinction in the late fourteenth century.

These two hills are part of a vast plateau of the Mounth of the Eastern Grampians encompassing a part of the watershed of streams feeding the Tay and the Dee. Of these and other adjacent heights Munro wrote that 'it is specially difficult to decide what are separate mountains, tops or merely shoulders'. Viewed across a major divide one can see why.

Below: Carn an Tuirc and Cairn of Claise from Carn Aosda (*Jim Teesdale*)

GLAS MAOL

3504ft/1068m Greenish-grey bare hill

One has only to tread the vast summit plain in mist in search of the summit cairn to realise that this hill is indeed well named and is another example of the Gaels' perception of the hill ground.

Glas Maol's lower slopes are the playground of the skier, the higher ground remaining the preserve of the mountaineer ever vigilant for the mists which frequently sweep its bald upland pate.

Left: Glas Maol from Creag Leacach (*Tom Rix*)

CREAG LEACACH

3238ft/987m Slabby rock

Smoothed ruffs of crag on an eastern flank should come as no surprise to a walker familiar with the Gaelic. The presence of stones on the ridge has been put to good use in the building of a boundary wall which can be followed across its scree scalp.

More frequently seen are the deep hollows of the slopes which border the sweep of the hill road climbing to the Devil's Elbow whether from the road or the hills to the west of it.

Above: Creag Leacach from The Cairnwell (*Irvine Butterfield*)

TOM BUIDHE

3140ft/957m Yellow knoll

Scarcely more than an undulation in the plateau which extends from Glen Shee across to Lochnagar, the colour of its tawny grasses is its most significant feature.

TOLMOUNT

3143ft/958m Valley hill, or hill of hollows

The name is a corruption of An Dul Monadh, the dul or dol mounth or hill. The word 'dul' or 'dol' here signifies Glen Doll. On the crossing of the Mounth this peak appears as a milestone announcing the start of the struggle to the high point of Jock's Road, an ancient hill crossing between Braemar and Glen Doll.

On approach from Glen Doll the two could be easily confused as they are identical twin points adjacent one to the other, and little more than ripples in an ocean of rolling hill-tops.

Left: Tom Buidhe and Tolmount from Cairn Damff (*Irvine Butterfield*)

CAIRN BANNOCH

3320ft/1012m Peaked hill

In the Gaelic this is Carn a' Beannaich, hill of the point, though the peak is little more than a stony height in a plain which has few points of interest other than the occasional cairn. In such a broad spread one hill is little different from another and Cairn Bannoch's cairn might easily pass without a second thought to its status.

BROAD CAIRN

3274ft/998m Hill of upland

This is another hill whose Anglicisation of the Gaelic 'Carn Braghaid' disguises its origins. Upland here signifies high land and the summit cairn lies on a broad cap on the edge of an upland spread, its one attractive view being that down Loch Muick.

Seen in the dying light of evening Cairn Bannoch seems almost a shadow of Broad Cairn whose status as a mountain seems the more assured by a more pronounced summit lump, enhanced by its proximity.

Below: Broad Cairn and Cairn Bannoch from Loch Muick (*Irvine Butterfield*)

MAYAR

3044ft/928m My delight, or the plain

The Gaelic names in this part of the Grampians have been very corrupted and the origins of this hill's name obscure. 'Magh ard', high plain, seems more appropriate than the alternative offering of 'M'aighear', signifying happiness, for its summit is but one high point in a plateau of glum peat-hags.

The mountain summit is best seen from the Glen Prosen side above Kilbo, a route used by those seeking an easier lift to its cairn than that from the steeper Glen Clova and Corrie Fee flank.

Above: South Craig and Mayar from Kilbo (*Irvine Butterfield*)

DRIESH

3107ft/947m Bramble place

The thorn or bramble of the Gaelic 'dris' may not be much in evidence these days as the lower slopes are clothed in conifers. The hill is a long established favourite of Dundonians who find sport in its Winter Corrie, and test their stamina on the stiff ascent by The Scorrie.

The great ridge of The Scorrie fills the near eastern horizon, a familiar rampart above a sea of conifers to those who tramp the ancient hill pass of Jock's Road on its climb from Glen Doll.

Left: Driesh from Jock's Road (*David May*)

LOCHNAGAR – CAC CARN BEAG

3789ft/1155m Little loch of noisy sound – Little hill of excrement

It seems odd that the mountain could do no better than be named after Lochan na Gaire in the north-east corrie. The original name for the mountain was Beinn nan Ciochan, hill of the paps, a reference to the nipples of the twin summit heights. The true summit name should more properly be Cadha Charn Beag, the little steep of the stony hill, but even this fails to give any hint of the majesty of its cliffs. These great crags often lie in shadow to substantiate Byron's descriptive 'steep frowning glories of dark Lochnagar' and it is this poetic imagery which led to the popular adoption of the present title.

Right: Lochnagar cliffs from the corrie (*Allen Fyffe*)

101

CARN AN T-SAGAIRT MOR

3435ft/1047m Big hill of the priest

The goodly cleric who gave this hill its title was Padruig of Braemar who led his flock to Glen Callater to pray for an end to a severe frost which had gripped the land into late spring. Their prayers were answered by a thaw and in their gratitude the local people named the hill after their priest. A well at the foot of Loch Callater is also a part of this tale which sets the mountain apart. It would otherwise be merely another height of passing interest on the great plateau stretching eastwards from the pass at the Devil's Elbow to the broad pate of Lochnagar.

Below: Carn an t-Sagairt Mor and Loch Callater from Morrone (*Irvine Butterfield*)

MOUNT KEEN

3081ft/939m Pleasant hill

The word mount here is the Gaelic 'monadh', a high moorland. The Mounth was formerly the name given to the high ground now known as the Grampians. Keen is a corruption of 'caoin', pleasant or gentle, and with a track across the shoulder of the hill the Munroist is assured of one of the easiest of ascents.

The most easterly Munro, its hill-top sits as an isolated pimple and from afar is the one identifiable landmark in the vast sea of a rumpled plateau – a true milestone of the moors.

Above: Mount Keen from the west (*Stuart Rae*)

MULLACH CLACH A' BHLAIR

3343ft/1019m Summit of the stone of the plain

The tumble of stones marking the summit of this hill lies at the southern end of the long ripple of hills which march above Glen Feshie and fringe the western bounds of the Moine Mhor, the great moss. The turn around the great bite of Coire Garbhlach announces the start of the final drag to the highest of the bland heights of this great plain.

Below: Looking across Coire Garbhlach to Mullach Clach a' Bhlair (*Jim Teesdale*)

WHITE MOUNTH

The Gaelic 'Am Monadh Geal' is an apt description of a flat summit crown of bleached stones which appears but a shoulder of the more famed Lochnagar.

CARN A' CHOIRE BOIDHEACH

3642ft/1110m Hill of the beautiful corrie

The corrie after which the summit is named relies on the sun's sparkle on the white stones to add enchantment to a scene forever captured by those who named and loved this spot.

The mountain and its eponymous corrie are best seen to advantage from the crag fringe of Creag an Dubh-loch. When cloaked in winter's snow it is truly the white mounth.

Above: The White Mounth from above Creag an Dubh-loch (*Iain A. Robertson*)

SGOR GAOITH

3668ft/1118m Peak of the wind

This summit, perched on an edge falling to Loch Einich, is subjected to the buffeting up-draughts caused by the gusty thermals rising against the crags hence its name, peak of the wind. Seen from local heights the mountain mass has twin heights of almost identical character, Sgor Gaoith only marginally higher than Sgoran Dubh.

Left: Sgor Gaoith from Creag an Leth-choin (*John Digney*)

BRAERIACH

4252ft/1296m Brindled or speckled upland

Occupying the largest area of ground above the 4000ft contour this mountain is a great upland sprawl. When viewed from Strath Spey the clouds scudding across the broad shoulders of the mountain give the heather-grasses a speckled appearance. This suggests that the people of Strath Spey named the hill rather than those on the Dee side who would have been tempted to praise its craggier corries overlooking the Lairig Ghru. An approach through the Rothiemurchus Forest takes advantage of the path to the Lairig Ghru and the lengthy ridge of Sron na Lairige above.

Right: Braeriach and the Lairig Ghru from Lurcher's Crag (*John Digney*)

CAIRN TOUL

4235ft/1291m Hill of the barn

As described in the Gaelic this is Carn an t-Sabhail, the most likely explanation being its barn-like shape when seen from the east. This contention appears to be supported by the presence of Coire an t-Sabhail on its north-eastern slope and the fact that locally it was sometimes called Sabhal Beinn Macdui, the barn of Ben Macdui.

Left: Cairn Toul from Sron Riach, Ben Macdui (*Iain A. Robertson*)

THE DEVIL'S POINT

3294ft/1004m

Bod an Deamhain, the penis of the demon, has been Anglicised in more discreet terminology. This in no way detracts from its commanding presence for when wet with rain its blackened face of slabs has about it an evil aura.

This impregnable image of the peak of Satan is put at nought by those who outflank it and attain the col for the level crown opens the way to an easy perambulation to the cairn.

Above: Approaching the summit of The Devil's Point (*Alan O'Brien*)

SGOR AN LOCHAIN UAINE

4127ft/1258m Peak of the little green loch

This peak sits as a high and short promontory above the deep hollow of a small tarn tinged a greenish hue by underwater plants and algae. The name The Angel's peak is a colloquial one and of fairly recent origin, said to have been given by those sensitive to the name attaching to the nearby peak associated with Lucifer.

A winter challenge for the cross-country skier is to do the round of the Cairngorm 4000ft peaks, the hardest part of the route being the ascent from the Lairig Ghru to the summit of Cairn Toul.

Left: Sgor an Lochain Uaine from Braeriach (*Irvine Butterfield*)

CARN A' MHAIM

3402ft/1037m Hill of the pass

When seen from Glen Luibeg the hill appears to have a rock nipple which would lend credence to the name being linked to a breast-shaped hill. However, the Gaelic 'mam', or 'mhaim' as here, can refer to a pass and as the hill stands at the entrance to the most famous pass of all, the Lairig Ghru, this seems more obvious to the majority of those who make the hill's acquaintance.

A look at the map suggested that this eminence might be considered more ridge than mountain. Seen from higher ground the nature of its lengthy spine is confirmed, which with the lazy dip to a col firmly establishes its distinctive identity.

Below: Carn a' Mhaim from Sron Riach, Ben Macdui (*Iain A. Robertson*)

MONADH MOR

3651ft/1113m Big hill or big moor

Given the proximity of greater heights and the vast spread of the high upland of which it forms a part its title is curious and simplistic. Large it may be when seen from the Geldie and such it must have appeared to those who formerly tended their flocks at the shielings thereabouts and gave it the original name, Am Monadh Mor.

BEINN BHROTAIN

3796ft/1157m Hill of the mastiff

Brodan was the legendary jet black hound of the Fingalians whose presence in the vicinity is also recorded in Coire Cath nam Fionn, the corrie of the battle of the Fingalians, enclosed in the angle between this hill and the neighbouring Monadh Mor. Ancient tales tell how Brodan came to grief when he chased the White Stag of Ben Alder into a loch in the Gaick, which now bears his name.

Carved from the one great plateau, such are their similarities of form that to differentiate between the two requires a point of vantage looking into the head of Glen Geusachan. Such view-points clearly reveal the dividing col above Coire Cath nam Fionn.

Right: Beinn Bhrotain and Monadh Mor from Sgor an Lochain Uaine (*Alan O'Brien*)

BYNACK MORE

3576ft/1090m Big shawl, kerchief or cap
Its original name was Beinn Beidhneag, the translation of which is obscure. On approaches from Strath Nethy the mountain appears to rise to a sharp point which for a Cairngorm mountain is unusual. This feature has been likened to the coif, or headgear, worn by women as a sign that they were married. In the Gaelic this is 'beannag', pronounced byanak.

From the north rock tors to the side of the summit might suggest chimneypots. In the Gaelic this is 'binneag', but bearing in mind that at the time Gaelic was spoken in the area many of the houses were without such ornament, and in the absence of other definitive translations, the romantic coif has the greater appeal.
Below: Summit of Bynack More from the north (*Allen Fyffe*)

BEN MACDUI

4294ft/1309m MacDuff's hill
More properly Beinn Mac, or Mhic, Duibh, literally translated as the hill of the son of the black one it may also be 'MacDuff's peak' as the MacDuff (MacDuibh) Earls of Fife once owned Mar Estate in which the mountain is situated. At a time when the hill was considered to be the highest in Scotland, the MacDuffs might have gained additional satisfaction in knowing that not only did they enjoy a royal neighbour but could also lay claim to the highest ground in their sovereign's kingdom. The summit is also quite literally the haunt of Am Fear Liath Mor, a giant spectre.
Above: Looking south-west to the summit of Ben Macdui (*Jim Teesdale*)

CAIRN GORM

4084ft/1245m Blue mountain

Most mountains when seen from a distance take on a bluish hue and this is the best known of several hills which have this name. The disappearance of the Gaelic in the locality has led to the name being adopted by the whole range which to the Gael was more properly Am Monadh Ruadh, the red mountain land, to distinguish it from the Monadhliath or grey mountain land on the opposite side of Strath Spey.

On a day of sun the reddish tinge of the summit rocks contrast with the dark blue of the crags on the mountain's corrie walls. These are undoubtedly the preserve of the cragsman and provide spectacle on the walk along the rims of Coire an t-Sneachda and Coire an Lochain away from the cacophonous summit of the mountain.

Right: Summit of Cairn Lochan, Cairn Gorm (*Ian Evans*)

BEINN MHEADHOIN

3878ft/1182m Middle mountain

Its central position in the Cairngorms massif soon becomes obvious to those who seek its summit tor for it is a long walk in from whatever the chosen access.

The tradition of the long walk in is of paramount consideration when tackling this peak for it lies central to the massif, hence the name signifying a 'hill in the middle'. Whether choosing the Glen Derry approach or that across the shoulder of Ben Macdui there is still the final pull to the summit tors, locally know as 'barns'.

Left: Beinn Mheadhoin from Ben Macdui (*Alan Fyffe*)

DERRY CAIRNGORM

3789ft/1155m The blue cairn of Derry

To the people of Glen Derry this was An Carn Gorm, the blue hill, later called Carn Gorm an Doire or Cairn Gorm of Derry when it became necessary to differentiate it from its larger counterpart above Strath Spey. Seen from Inverey the hill is quite distinctive and often appears dark blue in colour and looking much higher than Ben Macdui.

A short walk up Glen Ey provides the clearest view of the mountain above the remnant pines of the ancient forest of Caledonia. Here the slight gain in elevation above the settlement of Inverey gives the lie to the suggested superiority to Ben Macdui.

Below: Derry Cairngorm from Inverey (*Irvine Butterfield*)

BEINN BHREAC

3054ft/931m Speckled mountain

The speckled effect comes from the patches of scree which break up the heathery hillside above the Derry. One of the lowest of the Cairngorm Munros it does not detach itself significantly from the adjoining peaks. On approaches from Glen Derry or Glen Quoich it appears as a rather bland hill which provides an easy stepping off point for the high plateau of Beinn a' Bhuird, or Beinn a' Chaorainn.

Above: Looking up Glen Quoich to Beinn Bhreac (*Jim Teesdale*)

BEINN A' BHUIRD (NORTH TOP)

3927ft/1197m Table hill

Bianna bord is the old Dee-side Gaelic name for the hill whose great flat-topped summit resembles a huge table. The high-level walk from the southern to the northern top is one of contrast for on the western side slopes fall easily to the expansive moss of the Moine Bhealaidh whereas the eastern plunge of cliffs can startle with their verticality.

The mountain does not display its cliffs to full view until the summit ridge is reached and from a southern stance only a hint of their presence is given by the knot of A'Chioch.

Below: Beinn a' Bhuird from Morrone (*Irvine Butterfield*)

BEN AVON - LEABAIDH AN DAIMH BHUIDHE

3842ft/1171m Mountain of the ford of Fionn -The couch of the yellow stag

'Avon' could be derived from Athfhinn, 'the bright one', which here would refer to the River Avon. More romantically the title comes from Ath-fhinn, the water of Fingal. There is a ford Ath nam Fiann, ford of the Fingalians, and there is a tradition that here Fingal's wife fell on the slippery stones and was drowned. The name of the summit tor suggests this was a favourite resting place for a stag lighter in colouration than its fellows.

To appreciate the vast scale of this mountain find a vantage point high above Glen Clunie to the south, the better to see over the foothills about Braemar.

Right: Beinn a' Bhuird and Ben Avon from Glen Clunie (*Iain A. Robertson*)

BEINN A' CHAORAINN

3550ft/1082m Mountain of the rowan tree

If rowans exist on the slopes of this hill they are hard to find. This is another example of a popular hill name for there are many others associated with the mountain ash in the Highlands. There are few enthusiasts who readily identify with this particular hill as it sits in the shadow of too many grander peaks nearby. Nor is it easy to set the hill in the context of the Cairngorm giants as from most angles it has few features by which to delineate it. A sight of it along the Avon holds most promise.

Above: Beinn a' Chaorainn from Faindouran Lodge (*Richard Wood*)

THE WEST HIGHLANDS

THE WEST HIGHLANDS IS A LAND TYPIFIED BY LENGTHY GLENS STRETCHING westwards from the Great Glen to the western sea lochs of Nevis, Hourn and Duich. Steep-sided mountain ridges abound, with crag and corrie on every hand. This whole jumble of mountain ranges is a veritable paradise to those addicted to ridge walking, much of it above some of the lonely and loveliest of glens.

Left: Ladhar Bheinn from Druim Fada (*Paul Craven*)

MEALL NA TEANGA

3008ft/917m Round hill of the tongue

This hill forms a part of the mountain wall to the west of Loch Lochy, standing tall above the fringing pines of the South Laggan Forest. The tongue may refer to the steep buttressing spur rising from the loch to the hump of the summit.

The panorama of the Grey Corries and the peaks around Ben Nevis is further enhanced from summits poised above the deep rift of the Great Glen.

Left: Meall na Teanga from Sron a' Choire Ghairbh (*John Allen*)

SRON A' CHOIRE GHAIRBH

3067ft/935m Nose of the rough corrie

The mountain takes its name from Coire Garbh, tucked under the craggy nose in the angle between the hill and the outlier, Sean Mheall.

The scenic approach is that beside the stream above the waterfalls at the eastern end of Loch Arkaig, a route traversed long ago by cattle drovers *en route* from Skye. Nowadays walkers are grateful for the path which leads to the upper glen and a second hill crossing leading up to the gap under the great bulk of the mountain.

Below: Sron a' Choire Ghairbh from Gleann Cia-aig (*John Allen*)

GAOR BHEINN – GULVAIN

3238ft/987m Thrill, or filthy mountain

Keepers were said to shoot stags on the steep sides of the hill as by rolling down they saved the trouble of lengthy carry – a thrill for the keeper but not the stag! The name might equally be a corruption of the Gaelic 'gaoir', filthy, a possible reference to the greasy slabs on the steeper faces which hastened the deers' descent.

Munroists mindful that all approaches to the twin summits are steep and uncompromising regard the mountain with a grudging respect.

Above: Gulvain from Braigh nan Uamhachan (*Jim Teesdale*)

SGURR THUILM

3159ft/963m Peak of the rounded hillock
There are islets in the River Pean and at
one time the land around the head of
Loch Arkaig would be the rich flat land
beside the same river. Either
interpretation of the one time translation
of 'thuilm' as a holm would be appropriate
and suggests the hill was originally named
by those who dwelt on the mountain's
northern slopes. Given its distinctive
dome it is more likely that the name is
from 'tulach' signifying a rounded, or
knolly, hill. If from 'tolman' the hill has a
more magical quality as a knoll where
fairies' palaces lay concealed.
Left: Sgurr Thuilm from Sgurr nan
Coireachan (*Richard Wood*)

SGURR NAN COIREACHAN (PEAN)

3136ft/956m Peak of the corries
The name is an obvious one as this hill
possesses many fine corries on all flanks.

The greatest corrie is that at the head
of Glen Finnan below the sweep of the
ridge eastwards to Sgurr Thuilm, a useful
high level link to add encouragement to
complete a round of two fine peaks.
Right: Sgurr nan Coireachan from Druim
Coire a' Bheithe (*Ian Evans*)

SGURR NA CICHE

3412ft/1040m Pap-shaped peak or peak of the breast

Shape is the important element here and to the Gael would appear as the distinctive shape of a woman's breast.

GARBH CHIOCH MHOR

3323ft/1013m Big rough pap

Though not so obviously peaked as the neighbouring Sgurr na Ciche its name would more accurately be intended to link the two so that the alternative translation, big rough place of the breast, is probably the more accurate.

It is easy to see why the hills hereabouts attracted the name Garbh Criochan, the Rough Bounds, for rock is much in evidence. The construction of a wall along the crest attests to man's folly in pursuit of placing his own bounds upon Nature's masterpieces.

Left: Garbh Chioch Mhor and Sgurr na Ciche from Sgurr nan Coireachan (*Tom Rix*)

SGURR NAN COIREACHAN (DESSARRY)

3127ft/953m Peak of the corries

The people of Glen Dessarry obviously had similar thoughts about their peak to that of their kin in nearby Glen Pean, which is understandable given both peaks have their apex above several distinctive corries.

It is the greater corrie on the south which shapes the mountain summit, here seen from one of the approach ridges.

Right: Sgurr nan Coireachan of Glen Dessarry (*Alan O'Brien*)

122

GAIRICH

3015ft/919m Peak of yelling

The name is one of many associated with hunting and like several others suggests the presence of yelling or roaring stags. A direct descent denied by the waters of Loch Quoich sees the majority of approaches by a long eastern ridge which suddenly rears upwards to the summit. This is more deceptive than it looks from below and gives a final, short, sporting clamber along the edge of its eastern corrie rim.

Below: The eastern approach to Gairich's summit (*Jim Teesdale*)

SGURR MOR

3291ft/1003m Big peak

Compared to the adjacent mountains this peak stands up as a great stack and would be instantly recognised by those who once lived along the shores of Loch Quoich.

The shores are now uninhabited and those who travel west, or tackle the hills above the road along the loch's northern shore, might be forgiven if their attractions are diverted by the more shapely stack of Sgurr na Ciche at the head of the loch.

Above: Sgurr Mor and Loch Quoich from Coire Mheil (*Iain A. Robertson*)

MEALL BUIDHE

3104ft/946m Yellow lump or rounded
yellow hill

As most of the northern slopes are
composed of scarred rock, yellow is not a
colour one would immediately recognise
when applied to this hill. To those grazing
their cattle in the folds of Gleann
Meadail it would present a kinder face
and the grasses, or sunnier bowers, might
have thus found expression as these would
have a golden, or yellow, hue.

The mountain's twin tops have
extensive views and on a clear day beyond
and right of the conical Sgurr na Ciche
the dome of Ben Nevis is discerned on
the eastern horizon.

Below: Summit Meall Buidhe looking to
Sgurr na Ciche (*Tom Rix*)

LADHAR BHEINN

3346ft/1020m Forked mountain

Hoof or claw hill are the other suggested
origins of the name and as with 'forked'
draw attention to the ridge fingers which
run out from a central ridge.

This most westerly of the mainland
Munros is no stranger to mist whose
gradual clearance provides a stark
reminder of this mountain's awesome
majesty – a true throne of the gods.

Above: The spurs of Ladhar Bheinn from
the ridge (*Tom Rix*)

LUINNE BHEINN

3081ft/939m

The sea-swelling mountain

The normal interpretation of this hill's name is hill of anger, mirth or melody. There is a great deal of difference between anger and mirth and this ambiguity tends to suggest that the meaning of the hill's name lies elsewhere. Its proximity to the sea-lane of Loch Hourn and its shape reveals the possibility of a more romantic description likening it to a towering wave.

The effect of a rolling breaker may not be readily apparent when viewed from the landward side but a moment's reflection may suggest that the Gaelic vision is yet again an ever present theme.

Left: Luinne Bheinn from Mam Suidheig (*Irvine Butterfield*)

BEINN SGRITHEALL

3195ft/974m Scree of gravel hill

There is no doubt about this hill's name as from Arnisdale at its foot it seems to be one mass of scree rising to the ridge 3000ft above. Seen more distantly across the sound of Loch Hourn the unremitting climb from the shoreline is confirmed and it is obvious the hill is one to be reckoned with.

Below: Beinn Sgritheall from Creag Bheithe (*Irvine Butterfield*)

SGURR A' MHAORAICH

3369ft/1027m Peak of the shell fish

Molluscs found in the tidal reaches of Loch Hourn provide fare for sea-birds who might have been in the habit of depositing the broken shells on this hill's lower slopes. This seems a more plausible explanation of the hill's name than any reference to its shape.

Ascent from the east is by either of two ridges which meet at a summit knot looking down the fjord-like Loch Hourn to a distant Cuillin. It is this view which gives the hill its particular magic.

Right: Loch Hourn from Sgurr a' Mhaoraich (*Jim Teesdale*)

SPIDEAN MIALACH

3268ft/996m Peak of the louse

Mialach is often represented as wild animals but should more properly be from the Gaelic 'mialachas', lousiness. This may relate to the plagues of midges which are more prevalent here than elsewhere in the vicinity.

By providing the eastern views of loch and rolling hills this hill complements those of its near neighbour which looks to the rugged landscapes of the western heights.

Below: Spidean Mialach from Gleouraich (*Keith Pennyfather*)

CREAG A' MHAIM

3107ft/947m Crag of the breast

Like other hill names containing the word Mhaim, or Mam, this peak sits above a pass – that from Glen Cluanie to Glen Loyne – and this seems much the better interpretation of the hill's name, crag of the pass.

DRUIM SHIONNACH

3238ft/987m Ridge of the fox

This is one of the few hills with a specific mention of a fox. It may be that the hill was named in deference to a particularly cunning member of the genus which eluded capture.

There must be many a Munroist who has started out from Creag a' Mhaim to tackle the many listed peaks of the South Cluanie Ridge. Seen from the glen the second peak of the day seems hardly to merit separate mountain status which is perhaps as well as the others in the chain more than compensate for this illusion.

Right: Creag a' Mhaim and Druim Shionnach from Loch Cluaine (*Ian Evans*)

GLEOURAICH

3396ft/1035m Uproar or noise

Another mountain noted for its stags, many of which frequent the road along Loch Quoich-side, or whose roar echoes from the northern corrie walls during the rut.

The ascent of this peak can be decidedly easy as a pony track leads to a summit which is excuse enough to delay the descent to catch the last lingering moments of a setting sun.

Above: Loch Quoich from Gleouraich (*Richard Wood*)

AONACH AIR CHRITH

3350ft/1021m The shaking height

Also translated as trembling hill, there is a note of caution here as those who tread its airy blade will appreciate.

Winter only serves to emphasise the potential for excitement and this narrow section of the ridge may well be the highlight of the traverse of the greater ridge.

Left: Looking west to Aonach air Chrith (*Jim Teesdale*)

SGURR AN DOIRE LEATHAIN

3314ft/1010m

Peak of the broad thicket

There is no evidence of the thicket which helped single out this peak from those of similar structure, and at one time possibly supplied valuable timber for the inhabitants of Glen Shiel. Here a short turn of the ridge provides an opportunity to capture the opposing flanks of the mountain chain; buttressing crags to the north and the great bulge of convex slopes to the south falling into the mists rising in Wester Glen Quoich.

Left: Sgurr an Doire Leathain from Sgurr an Lochain (*Richard Wood*)

MAOL CHINN-DEARG

3218ft/981m Bald red-headed hill

Ordnance Survey maps give the title to the narrow ridge connected to Aonach air Chrith which is clearly erroneous as its bald lump sits at the western end of this delicate promenade.

Above: Maol Chinn-dearg from Glen Shiel (*Irvine Butterfield*)

CREAG NAN DAMH

3012ft/918m Rock of the stags

Another mountain with hunting links and a name not inappropriate even today. For many who tackle the South Cluanie Ridge this is the final summit of the east-west traverse. Tired limbs face a final challenge on the steep decline of the ridge to the road in Glen Shiel.

Below: Creag nan Damh from the east (*Richard Wood*)

THE SADDLE

3314ft/1010m

One of the few mountains with an English name, a clear reference to the shape of the summit when seen from Glen Shiel. To be savoured is the soaring blade of the Forcan Ridge, considered one of the finest ascent routes in the West Highlands. The exposed height of its narrow *arête* adds to the thrill of the expanding view eastwards along the deep trench of Glen Shiel.

Right: The Forcan Ridge of The Saddle (*Jim Teesdale*)

SGURR AN LOCHAIN

3294ft/1004m Peak of the little loch

This is the only peak of the chain known as the Cluanie Ridge which sits above a tarn so that the name is an obvious means of distinguishing the mountain from its peers.

Walkers attempting the traverse of the South Cluanie Ridge will be firmly in their stride by the time this peak is reached, westward progress here plotted by the posts of an old fence along the ridge.

Above: Sgurr an Lochain from the east (*Alan O'Brien*)

Even so the mountain detaches itself from neighbouring heights and has interest enough to warrant a second look.

Below: Sgurr na Sgine from the Barrisdale path (*Irvine Butterfield*)

SGURR FHUARAN

3501ft/1067m Odhran's peak

Several streams issue from the higher slopes and these may have given rise to a suggestion that the peak was noted for its wells or springs. The proper title of the mountain should be Sgurr Urain, the peak of Odhran, a kinsman and follower of Columba who was buried on the sacred island of Iona.

SGURR NA CARNACH

3287ft/1002m The peak of the stony ground

As the rockiest summit of the celebrated Five Sisters and possessed of no other obvious attributes it simply became noted for its terrain.

Easily distinguished by their steep ribs and deep dividing gullies these two pyramidal peaks are much in evidence from Shiel Bridge and along the shores of Loch Duich.

Right: Sgurr Fhuaran and Sgurr na Carnach from Loch Duich (*Ian Evans*)

SGURR NA CISTE DUIBHE

3369ft/1027m Peak of the black chest

After the battle of Glen Shiel (1719) a party of Spanish mercenaries escaped up the adjacent hill, which is named after them. Though some of the coins they dropped were later found there is no mention that they fell from a black chest. Romantic though it might be to consider such a link the black chest is in reality the deep hollow of the Allt Dearg on the south-west slope.

Sgurr na Ciste Duibhe is the fifth in line of the Five Sisters and marks the turn of the ridge. When approached from the east an airy view is to be had across Glen Shiel to The Saddle.

Above: Sgurr na Ciste Duibhe and Sgurr nan Spainteach from Beinn Odhar (*Ian Evans*)

SGURR NA SGINE

3104ft/946m Peak of the knife

The defending crags of the eastern flank lie cross-wise to the ridge which links the mountain to the peaks of the South Cluanie Ridge. When viewed from the east this wall of rock under the summit ridge has a blade-like quality which could explain the name given. This is less obvious when viewed from other angles.

SAILEAG

3136ft/956m Little heel

The little heel is that part of the ridge pointing west as there is a more prominent one, Meall a'Charra, striking north from the summit.

SGURR A' BHEALAICH DHEIRG

3399ft/1036m Peak of the red gap

The summit cairn is a fine example of the stonemason's art and sits a little north-east of the main line of the long ridge north of Glen Shiel. Just north of the summit the ridge out towards Fionngleann is cut by a reddish gully, a gap whose uniqueness lends itself to the mountain's name.

Looking east from the Five Sisters the long ridge running above Glen Cluanie reaches its high point on Sgurr a' Bhealaich Dheirg.

Above right: Saileag and Sgurr a' Bhealaich Dheirg from Sgurr nan Spainteach (*Ian Evans*)

CISTE DHUBH

3212ft/979m Black chest

A display of black crags under the summit probably accounts for the name though the play of light upon the heather or dark corners may be of equal significance.

The mountain is separated from neighbours on all sides by deep dividing glens or well-defined dips in connecting ridges.

Right: Ciste Dhubh from Bealach a' Choinich (*John Digney*)

AONACH MEADHOIN

3284ft/1001m Middle ridge

This summit lies at the centre of a ridge possessing one large and one lesser hump so that topography played a part in the naming of this elevation.

Seen from Strath Cluanie the peak is shielded by its satellite top, Sgurr an Fhuarail, whose graceful decline is complemented by that of adjacent Corbett, Am Bathach.

Left: Aonach Meadhoin and Am Bathach from Strath Cluanie (*Jim Teesdale*)

MULLACH FRAOCH-CHOIRE

3615ft/1102m Top of the heather corrie

As the heather corrie lies under the mountain's northern slopes it seems certain that the peak was a significant landmark to those who once tended the shielings in Glen Affric.

A'CHRALAIG

3674ft/1120m The basket or creel

A tarn, a corrie and a stream all with creel in their name suggest that the corrie most resembled a creel with the mountain taking its name from the great hollow beneath it.

Seen in profile from the east the two mountains display the corries and crags which are their finest features, an isolated top, A'Chioch, also revealing the individualistic stature which led to its name.

Above right: A'Chralaig and Mullach Fraoch-choire from Carn a' Choire Ghairbh (*Jim Teesdale*)

SAIL CHAORAINN

3287ft/1002m Heel of the rowan trees

The name is more properly that of the spur from the main north-south ridge of this massif. Until recent editions of *Munro's Tables* this hill was known as Tigh Mor na Seilge, the big house of hunting, which is more in keeping with the great boss of its summit, as witnessed by similar connections with hunting dogs on the adjacent mountain. The hill lies very much in the shadow of its higher companion both physically and in the mind of those seeking out the Munro summits, a fact often illustrated on a winter's day when the sun at its zenith barely touches the crags of an eastern hollow.

Left: Sail Chaorainn from Sgurr nan Conbhairean (*Jim Teesdale*)

138

SGURR NAN CONBHAIREAN

3638ft/1109m Peak of the dog men

This hill may have been one where the keeper of the hounds rested or used to spy out the land. Its first recorded ascent was that of the fugitive Bonnie Prince Charlie on 23 July 1746 on a day thick with midges. In the vicinity he met up with the Seven Men of Glenmoriston and found sanctuary in the cave of Coiregoe, the hollow to the north-east.

An impressive bulwark of eastern cliffs is exposed to view on the approach from the south by way of an attendant Carn Ghluasaid, often climbed as a precursor to the traverse of this eastern end of the Cluanie horseshoe.

Right: Sgurr nan Conbhairean from Carn Ghluasaid (*Richard Wood*)

CARN GHLUASAID

3140ft/957m Hill of movement

It cannot escape the visitor that the cairn lies at the crumbling edge of Coire Sgreumh, the corrie of gloom. It is the movement of the unstable screes on this northern wall which gave the hill its name rather than the tendency of the cairn to slip over the edge.

Travellers passing by are conscious only of a broad hill flank of wild heath and scoured stone which excites little attention. Even when the sun shines it seems an uninviting prospect except to the hill-walker in search of its lonely cairn.

Left: Carn Ghluasaid from Cluanie dam (*Irvine Butterfield*)

A' GHLAS-BHEINN

3012ft/918m The greenish-grey mountain

There might have been more dramatic names to give a mountain whose steep slopes, as presented to the Loch Duich, are seamed with gullies. Its greenish-grey hue seems to have appealed more to those who named it, suggesting that it held a place in the lives of the people who formerly dwelt in and around the head of Glen Affric.

Below: A' Ghlas-bheinn from Sgurr Gaorsaic (*Jim Teesdale*)

BEINN FHADA – BEN ATTOW

3386ft/1032m Long mountain

A ridge five miles long above the 2000ft contour and a walk along the lower slopes of some eight miles quickly indicates the perceptions of those who named this mountain.

Lying between two passes, each leading to the remote head of Glen Affric it can be truly said that the mountain lies at the 'gates of Affric'. With unimpeded views along both sides of this glen the compass of mountains ranged on either hand is most extensive.

Right: Looking south-east from the summit of Ben Attow (*Irvine Butterfield*)

SGURR NAN CEATHREAMHNAN

3776ft/1151m Peak of the quarters

The quarters are shares of land claimants though it may equally have been due to a meeting of four distinct ridges. Even today three estate boundaries have their meeting on the summit ridge.

AN SOCACH

3022ft/921m The snout

This mountain is overshadowed by the higher peaks to east and west so that it does not have presence. The snout is most likely to be the nose above Bealach Coire Ghaidheil to the east, as its southern nose is separately named An Sornach, the long-chinned.

The higher peak dominates the head of Glen Affric, and when seen across that glen it is possible to make out the smaller An Socach as a culmination of the arm of An Sornach rising as backdrop to Coire Ghaidheil, a dark re-entrant above the lochan set in the river flats.

Left: Sgurr nan Ceathreamhnan and An Socach from Carn a' Choire Ghairbh (*Jim Teesdale*)

MULLACH NA DHEIRAGAIN

3222ft/982m Summit of the kestrel

This mountain is another which has suffered at the hands of the cartographers who once chose to name it Creag a' Choir' Aird, rock of the high corrie. Its new appellation may come from 'deargan-allt', the kestrel, a bird with reddish plumage. This has more appeal than the alternative interpretation, redder round hill.

Sgurr nan Ceathreamhnan throws out lengthy ridges to the north of which the easterly of the two is a mountain in its own right. Appearing as a long tail to the parent peak might be said by the Munroist to have a sting in it – it is a long diversion out to the cairn.

Left: Mullach na Dheiragain from the east ridge of Sgurr nan Ceathreamhnan (*Alan O'Brien*)

MAM SODHAIL

3875ft/1181m Round hill of the barns

Seen from Affric the mountain has a shape similar to that of Cairn Toul in the Cairngorms and this might account for the name. It might also be that the shielings in Coire Leachavie had small adjacent barns with like significance, as on this approach the mountain appears as a large rounded summit which seems to substantiate the connection with this corrie.

Everything about Mam Sodhail is on the grand scale with even its satellite tops bearing the hallmark of mountains. An eastern outlier, Sgurr na Lapaich was originally considered to be such by Munro.

Above: Sgurr na Lapaich ridge from the summit of Mam Sodhail (*Jim Teesdale*)

TOM A' CHOINICH

3645ft/1111m Pointed hill of the moss

A crown of moss on this undulation of the ridge stretching from Toll Creagach to Carn Eige easily explains the name.

A path by Gleann nam Fiadh up to a pass under the peak's eastern prow introduces a finely sculpted hill which quite belies its title.

Above: Tom a' Choinich from Gleann nam Fiadh (*Jim Teesdale*)

CARN EIGE – CARN EIGHE

3881ft/1183m Cairn of the notch or file

There is certainly a pronounced notch separating this peak from the twin Mam Sodhail. Equally, a long eastern ridge with several broken rock teeth might give rise to the presumption that Eige is more properly Eighe, a file.

It is this long eastern ridge which provides the high promenade with the objective peak tantalisingly distant from fellow Munro, Tom a' Choinich.

Opposite: An Leth-chreag and Carn Eighe from Tom a' Choinich (*John Allen*)

BEINN FHIONNLAIDH

3297ft/1005m Finlay's mountain

This mountain takes its name from 'Fionnla Dubh nam Fiadh', Black Findlay of the deer. An archer of the Clan MacRae, he was a retainer of the MacKenzies of Gairloch in charge of the deer forest of Glen Cannich. One day on the hill Findlay encountered a clansman of the MacDonald of Glengarry whose presence he challenged. Resistance being offered, Findlay shot the intruder. Glengarry sent twelve men to avenge his kinsman but all but one were poisoned by Findlay's wife. The survivor informed his chief, who sent a further dozen men. Findlay killed them one by one, and followed this exploit with the dispatch of a further dozen MacDonalds who overtook him on a hill above Glen Elchaig. The MacDonalds were finally avenged by an itinerant doctor of the clan who treacherously implanted a needle in Findlay's brain as he lay ill at Faddoch. These exploits date from the 1580s and if, as seems highly likely, Findlay slew his opponent on the hill, record the first ascent of a Scottish 3000ft peak.

To some Munroists the mountain seems as irascible as its eponymous namesake, and often despairing comment identifies those who have chosen to push on from Carn Eige to the more prestigious height of Mam Sodhail on their rounds of the demanding ranges of Affric. Long spring days or those of early summer are best for such ambitious hill-days.

Right: Beinn Fhionnlaidh from 'Seldom Inn' (*Irvine Butterfield*)

TOLL CREAGACH

3455ft/1053m Rocky hollow

The rocky hollow lies under the summit on the northern slopes above Loch Mullardoch and is the one feature of an otherwise undistiguished hump of a mountain.

The broad easy slopes to this easterly outlier of the northern ridge bounding Glen Affric are often precursors to a traverse westwards to Beinn Eige and Mam Sodhail, or a short carefree day by way of the Bealach Toll Easa.

Left: Toll Creagach from Bealach Toll Easa (*John Allen*)

SGURR NA LAPAICH

3773ft/1150m Peak of the bog

A curious name for so shapely a peak. The boggiest ground lies in the southern hollow or it could equally relate to the northern folds.

It is as a view-point that the mountain excels with views on every hand to the great ranges of Affric and Mullardoch and on a clear day a possible glimpse of distant Ben Nevis.

Right: Braigh a' Choire Bhig from Sgurr na Lapaich (*Keith Pennyfather*)

CARN NAN GOBHAR

3254ft/992m Hill of the goats

One of several mountains where goats were once prevalent and were hunted long ago for their meat and hides. The mountain is more view-point than a peak of any prominence, its flat top ideal for surveying the vast tracts of country around remote Loch Monar.

Left: Loch Monar from Carn nan Gobhar (*Keith Pennyfather*)

SGURR NA RUAIDHE

3258ft/993m Peak of the redness

The redness may well refer to the colour of the deer but more probably the heather of which there are vast acres along the hill's flanks, neighbouring hills having a greener look.

CARN NAN GOBHAR

3254ft/992m Hill of the goats

Goats must have roamed extensively in the hills about Strathfarrar as this is the second hill in the area which bears the same title.

Distance lends some enchantment to a view of these well-rounded twins set in the wild country between Monar and the Orrin. Access is eased by a stalkers' path along the corridor of Coire Mhuillidh, a precious aid when time to explore is limited by the gate-keeper at the foot of the glen.

Right: Carn nan Gobhar and Sgurr na Ruaidhe from Sgorr na Diollaid (*Jim Teesdale*)

AN RIABHACHAN

3704ft/1129m The brindled one

The play of light upon this hill's great flanks, and the speckled effect of the stone-studded turf are features which immediately spring to mind when seeking an explanation for this hill-name.

Flecked with remnants of snow it displays both the steepness of a northern flank and one of the twists at the end of its flat-topped crest.

Above: An Riabhachan from Sgurr na Lapaich (*John Allen*)

AN SOCACH

3507ft/1069m The snout

This hill ought to be better known as Meall a' Chaisg as this nomenclature has the greater prominence on the larger scale Ordnance Survey maps. The Gaelic 'caisg' can refer to Easter and it could be that long ago some religious ceremony connected with that festival was performed in the shadow of this hill.

This is undeniably one of the remoter Munros as it sits at the end of a chain on the divide between the glens of

Mulladoch and Monar. In appearance it displays a somewhat shapeless bulk requiring sight of an eastern snout to assist in its identification from a distance.

Right: An Socach and Loch Cruoshie from Beinn Dronaig (*Tom Rix*)

SGURR A' CHOIRE GHLAIS

3553ft/1083m Peak of the greenish-grey corrie

The choice of name is prosaic and is taken from the grey-green hollows on the southern slopes which suggests that former inhabitants of Glen Strathfarrar named the hill. The hollows shape the summit whose short crest sports a fine cairn and Ordnance Survey pillar suggesting that this mountain's central position is a favoured view-point.

Left: Sgurr a' Choire Ghlais across Coire Glas Mor (*Jim Teesdale*)

SGURR FHUAR-THUILL

3441ft/1049m Peak of the cold hollow

The tarn of a northern corrie sees little sun for much of the year and as the peak casts its shadow so the name of the baleful waters is reflected in the chosen name for this hill.

Most westerly of the four hills in the chain to the north of Glen Strathfarrar it is also the most difficult to attain, and in so remote a setting the companionship of a kindred spirit is to be welcomed.

Right: Sgurr Fhuar-thuill from Sgurr a' Choire Ghlais (*David McLeod*)

MORUISG

3044ft/928m Big water

This name conjures up visions of rolling sea breakers which is a somewhat poetic picture of this hill's stature as the highest point in a rambling range of rounded hills.

SGURR NAN CEANNAICHEAN

3002ft/915m Peak of the merchants or pedlars

Why the itinerant merchants should give their name to this hill goes unrecorded. At a time when the main route from east to west lay by way of Strathconon it may have been regarded as a significant milestone on the long journey between the townships of east and west.

Easily linked, these two hills are in the lower echelons of the Munro stable yet with attractions to cause a walker pause to remember the display of light and cloud about them after a day on lesser summits nearby.

Left: Moruisg and Sgurr nan Ceannaichean from Sgurr na Feartaig (*Irvine Butterfield*)

MAOILE LUNNDAIDH

3304ft/1007m Bare hill of the wet place

This hill lies on a catchment of the Conon and Monar with an abundance of high-level lochans to catch the snow-melt and summer rains. As such all its hollows are damp confined places.

So level is the summit plain that the actual high point has been a matter for conjecture, and only in relatively recent times have maps confirmed that the cairn at the northern end of the broad ridge has it by the smallest of margins. This lacks the virtue of the old summit of Creag Toll a' Choin which has the better view down Loch Monar to the east.

Right: Loch Monar from Creag Toll a' Choin, Maoile Lunndaidh (*Richard Wood*)

BIDEIN A' CHOIRE SHEASGAICH

3100ft/945m

Peak of the barren or milkless cattle

As the little peak of the reedy corrie from the Gaelic 'seasg', sedge, the interpretation would be equally apt as no cattle could be expected to yield milk on such poor ground. To those unfamiliar with the Gaelic the latter word in its title is often phonetically rendered as 'cheesecake'.

LURG MHOR

3235ft/986m

Big shank

The shank, or ridge stretching into the plain, well describes the lengthy ridge which the mountain extends towards Loch Monar.

Remote and difficult of access, with protection afforded by other mountain barriers, the attainment of their respective cairns is the preserve of the determined as the prospect from hills on the periphery of their sanctuary will confirm.

Right: Lurg Mhor, Bidein a' Choire Sheasgaich and Beinn Tharsuinn from Sgurr na Feartaig (*Irvine Butterfield*)

SGURR A' CHAORACHAIN

3455ft/1053m Peak of the little field of berries

Older maps gave the name Sgurr a' Chaoruinn, hill of the rowan. Nowadays it is not significantly rich in rowans and there are no fields of berries either. These vicissitudes apart it still retains a commanding presence.

SGURR CHOINNICH

3277ft/999m Mossy peak

A northern edge of crag and narrow rough ridge might have elicited a characteristic description. Perhaps the mossy connotations were intended to warn that a slip on the greasy surface could prove disastrous.

The natural features of these twinned mountains and their connecting ridge are on display and more apparent to observers on ascents to the Bealach Bhearnais or from Sgurr na Feartaig.

Above: Sgurr a' Chaorachain and Sgurr Choinnich from Sgurr na Feartaig (*Jim Teesdale*)

THE NORTH-WEST HIGHLANDS

THE FOUNDATION UPON WHICH MOST OF THE MOUNTAINS OF THE NORTH-WEST Highlands is built is one of the oldest in the world. Many of the mountains themselves are the eroded remains of Torridon sandstone which has weathered to form great stacks which heave themselves skyward from moors littered with lochans. In the far north lie some of the wildest and most isolated areas in Britain, the great sprawling ranges often the one sure boundary of vast deer forests in a country now cleared of its people.

Left: An Teallach ridge from Sgurr Fiona (*Paul Craven*)

MAOL CHEAN-DEARG

3061ft/933m Bald red-headed hill

The baldness is indeed acute, a great mass of reddish scree and rock which litters the upper slopes.   In shape the mountain is unmistakably a large dome planted firmly on the bedrock of Torridon sandstone. From whichever angle you look at it this mountain impresses.

Left: Maol Chean-dearg from Beinn Damh (*Clarrie Pashley*)

BEINN LIATH MHOR

3035ft/925m Big grey, or hoary, mountain

Beards of grey scree mark this hill out from the neighbouring Munros and with three summits to its ridge it is a hill of some size as the name implies. Size here would appear to imply length which is revealed to those on the approach to the mountain sanctuary of Coire Lair.

Above: Beinn Liath Mhor from Coire Lair (*John Digney*)

SGORR RUADH

3156ft/962m Red peak

The red Torridon sandstone is much in evidence on the buttresses and crags which add to the grandeur of this mountain.

   Step back a little to appreciate the shapeliness of its peak, now the better seen from several outlooks along the new road south of Loch Carron.

Right: Sgorr Ruadh across Strath Carron from Cam-allt (*Irvine Butterfield*)

BEINN ALLIGIN

Mountain of beauty or jewel mountain

The nearest Gaelic word to the current spelling is 'ailleagan', a jewel or darling. The whole mountain name is much more attractive as a title than that conferred on its highest point, for it is a jewel in every sense of the word.

SGURR MHOR

3231ft/985m Big peak

The great cleft which slices the face of this peak might have suggested a more evocative name so that the mere appellation of 'big peak' scarce does justice to so soaring and attractive a view-point, the equal of its peers in every respect.

TOM NA GRUAGAICH

3025ft/922m Mound of the maiden or damsel

Whoever the lady who gave her name to this hill she would have in all probability been one of rare beauty which quite appropriately complements the greater mountain's title. 'Gruagach' may also refer to a bride's maid of honour or a supernatural being.

One does not have to be a mountaineer to appreciate the jewel that is Beinn Alligin and motorists can have no cause for complaint as some of the finest views to be had are from the road to the south of Loch Torridon.

Left: Beinn Alligin from Dubh Aird
(Ian Evans)

LIATHACH

Grey or hoary place

The name comes from 'Liaghach' or 'An Liaghach' suggesting its hoary screes were of most interest to those who lived within the mountain's shadow. Gazing at this awesome mountain one has cause to wonder why grey was considered the dominant colour as the immediate impression is one of a series of russet rock terraces rising majestically from the floor of Glen Torridon.

SPIDEAN A' CHOIRE LEITH

3458ft/1054m Pinnacle of the grey corrie

More correctly the name to the Gael is Spiodan a' Choire Leith. The highest of the summits takes its name from the grey scree bowl tucked immediately beneath a magnificent prow outthrust from the summit cone.

MULLACH AN RATHAIN

3356ft/1023m Top of the pulley wheels

Some interpretations give the name as summit of the row of pinnacles. These could be either of two groups, those central to the mountain's crest known as Am Fasarinen, the passes, or those of the northern ridge of Meall Dearg, the red rounded hill, which buttresses this peak.

Liathach is impressive guardian of the northern bounds of Glen Torridon, a real giant of a mountain. Even when seen from a high vantage point the abiding memory is of a mountain citadel with few equals.

Right: Liathach and Glen Torridon from Sgurr Dubh (*Alan O'Brien*)

BEINN EIGHE

Mountain of the file

Pale screes glinting in the sun give the impression that this mountain range is coated in ice which some have deduced to be the interpretation of the mountain's name as one of ice. Its lengthy ridge as seen from Kinlochewe has a jagged edge to it known as the 'Black Carls'. This helps in the correct choice of title, mountain of the file.

SPIDEAN COIRE NAN CLACH

3258ft/993m Pinnacle of the corrie of stones

With hoary screes much in evidence on Beinn Eighe it comes as no surprise to find that one of its many corries is 'one of stones'. That a peak takes a similar title is neither complimentary nor derogatory, merely a statement of fact. Stones abound on its summit which enjoys a central position on the serpentine ridge of this deservedly popular range.

To the casual bystander this peak might be mistaken for the summit. The high point presented to the Torridon road is grand enough to excite the attention of those who pass that way.

Left: Beinn Eighe from Loch Clair
(*Ian Evans*)

RUADH-STAC MOR (BEINN EIGHE)

3314ft/1010m Big, or larger, red steep hill

Curiously the highest point lies hidden behind the main ridge and though given a name suggesting that it is red such a title could only be justified from the underlying stratum as its cap is of grey stones. These have sent down cascades of scree allowing for entertaining scrambles through the rocks to gain the cairn on a magnificent summit prow.

Left: Ruadh-stac Mor from the main ridge, Beinn Eighe (*Jim Maison*)

SLIOCH

3218ft/981m The spear place

From the Gaelic 'An sleaghach', or 'slaighaich', which suggests that those who named it were aware that its impressive tower took the form of a massive arrowhead, a shape not immediately recognised from Loch Maree's shores.

Add a touch of the relict pines of the old Caledonian forest and the mountain appears as unchanged as it was when man first came this way.

Right: Slioch from Grudie Bridge (*Ian Evans*)

BEINN TARSUINN

3074ft/937m Transverse or crosswise
mountain

This mountain sits at the head of Gleann
na Muice and links two parallel ridges
either side of that glen and thus lies
crosswise to them. In the original *Munro's
Tables* it was listed as a mountain at 3080ft
as the Scottish Mountaineering Club
members were more diligent in their
surveys than staff of the Ordnance Survey.
A note by Mr Colin Philip to the revised
tables of 1921 commented, 'the map of
this part was very casual; I think the OS
had bad weather, and was hurried in order
to meet the views of the then laird'.

The most noteworthy feature of this
mountain is the table, a flat-topped knot
on its western ridge.

Right: Beinn Lair and Gleann Tulacha
from Beinn Tarsuinn (*Jim Teesdale*)

A'MHAIGHDEAN

3172ft/967m The maiden
The profile of the mountain as seen from
the west might be likened to that of a
bound stook of corn. By tradition the
Highlanders called the last sheaf of corn
to be cut at harvest the maiden, and so
grand a hill would hold an especial
attraction to those who lived beneath it.

RUADH STAC MOR

3012ft/918m Big, or larger, steep red hill
Worn terraces of Torridon sandstone are
the obvious hallmark of this hill which
long suffered at the hands of the

cartographers, so that it was not until the
metric revision of the maps that its 3000ft
status was confirmed.

By contrast, views from the east
show a distinct difference in shape, the
craggy A'Mhaighdean's lines softened by
a broad flank, whereas it is Ruadh Stac
Mor which appears the more difficult hill
to climb.

Above: A'Mhaighdean and Ruadh
Stac Mor from Beinn Tarsuinn
(*Ralph Storer*)

BEINN A' CHLAIDHEIMH

3005ft/916m Mountain of the sword
The narrowness of this mountain's crest may account for the name, but remembering that at least one loch is named after a sword thrown into it after settlement of a land-holding dispute perhaps there is a more romantic story to be told about how this hill came by its title.

The narrow blade of its ridge is best seen from neighbouring Sgurr Ban and with a little photographic ingenuity the mountain can assume a stature normally denied.
Below: Beinn a' Chlaidheimh from Sgurr Ban (*Ralph Storer*)

SGURR BAN

3245ft/989m Pale peak
The summit of this hill is liberally covered with white quartzite blocks so that on acquaintance the name seems most logical. In sunlight the bleached stones are the whitest on any Scottish hill.

MULLACH COIRE MHIC FHEARCHAIR

3343ft/1019m Top of the son of Farquhar's corrie
The first Earl of Ross, Farquhar Macintaggart, had a son William who was a great hunter. It is this son, who acceded to the title in 1251, who is said to have given his name to the corrie beneath the hill. In turn the named hollow gave title to the hill above it.

These peaks are a part of the eastern leg of six Munros which form a horseshoe around Gleann na Muice in the heart of the Fisherfield Forest, an area remote of access and commonly regarded as Scotland's last great wilderness.

Above: Sgurr Ban and Mullach Coire Mhic Fhearchair from Beinn Tarsuinn (*Iain A. Robertson*)

AN TEALLACH

The Forge

The name the forge is said to derive from the glow of the sun on the vapours rising from the corrie, the jagged teeth of the ridge then appearing in the imagination as the embers in the local Dundonnell smiddy fire. Others say that the name recalls a time when tinkers fashioned their pots and pans on a small forge in the great bowl of an eastern corrie.

SGURR FIONA

3478ft/1060m Peak of wine

The name may be derived from the Gaelic 'fionn', light-coloured, but such a designation appears false as it is no different in hue from other peaks in the range. Thomas Pennant was an inheritor of estates in Flintshire, a considerable wealth which allowed him to indulge his passion for travel and natural history. On his tour of Scotland in 1772 he was informed that the crags were called Sgur-fein, or hills of wine, which seems to point to the rich ruby colour of the crags which buttress this elegant height.

Left: An Teallach from Loch Droma
(*David May*)

BIDEIN A' GHLAS THUILL (AN TEALLACH)

3484ft/1062m Sharp peak of the greenish-grey hollow

This, the highest point of An Teallach, takes its name from the deep recess of an eastern corrie whose grasses often lie in the shadow of cascades of grey scree; hence the green and the grey.

An Teallach is a range which appears in all its glory when the early morning sun lights up the crags above its eastern corrie. Travellers early on the road to Ullapool see the impressive mountain as they cross the Dirrie More. Mountaineers may claim it as their preserve, but this mountain greets everyone with equal uplift of the spirit.

SGURR BREAC

3277ft/999m Speckled peak

As with other mountains of the name the speckled effect comes from the hill's features. In this case it is the rock-studded slopes which when caught by the sun give the looked-for effect.

The mountain fills the skyline seen from the road, built to provide work in time of hardship. On the rise to the most exposed moors about the 'Destitution Road', and in the fading light of day, some semblance of sparkle might be detected on the craggy heights.

Below: Sgurr Breac from Abhainn Culeig bridge (*Irvine Butterfield*)

A' CHAILLEACH

3271ft/997m The old woman

Said by a keeper resident at Lochivroan in the 1920s to be named due to its likeness to an old dame at work. There may also be a link to the legendary Cailleach Bheur but in the absence of any tales handed down, who can say!

The old lady's apron of decaying birches are evidence of the degradation of a landscape which once rang to the voices of the people in the glen at its foot. Apart from the keeper on his beat these hills are the preserve of the backpacker seeking out these intimate corners on the fringes of an interior now devoid of inhabitants.

Above: A'Chailleach across Loch a' Bhraoin (*Jim Teesdale*)

SGURR NAN EACH

3028ft/923m Peak of the horses

The name of the hill speaks of a time when horses roamed free. This would be a location known to the Highlanders for the animals to be found there. Seen from the low ground the mountain can appear as little more than a spur of the higher Sgurr nan Clach Geala, and an obvious approach to it. On such a round of these two hills the retrospective view from the higher peak shows the gracious curve of the linking ridge, with buttressing crags adding to a more appealing prospect.

Below: Sgurr nan Each from Sgurr nan Clach Geala (*Jim Teesdale*)

SGURR NAN CLACH GEALA

3586ft/1093m Peak of the white stones

The name of the hill is self-explanatory once you locate the white stones near the summit, for these would provide a useful point of reference, and still do.

In winter the snow-plastered crags bring to the hill their own particular brand of whiteness which on a clear day provides ample excuse to linger at the cairn before pressing on.

Right: Summit of Sgurr nan Clach Geala (*Lorraine Nicholson*)

MEALL A' CHRASGAIDH

3064ft/934m Hill of the crossing

The crossing here is that between Loch a' Bhraoin and Loch Fannich and the hill lies at the northern portal of this one decent gap in the Fannichs range.

Easy access by a north-western ridge makes this a popular route to and from the western end of the Fannich massif centred on Sgurr Mor. The prospect of the hills ranged about Loch a' Bhraoin and the western prospect of the mighty An Teallach constantly in view are excuse enough to linger on the descent.

Above: Loch a' Bhraoin and An Teallach from Meall a' Chrasgaidh (*Alan O'Brien*)

SGURR MOR

3642ft/1110m Big peak

The highest point of the Fannichs, seen from a distance as a sharp-tipped cone. The name gives some indication of the mountain's significance as a landmark since no other in the range stands out so prominently.

The attainment of Sgurr Mor's crowning summit is the key to a day's outing in the Fannichs, and from the lower eastern tops it is a spur to achievement on the short days of winter when crisp snow speeds the traverse to its summit.

Left: Sgurr Mor from the east (*Alan O'Brien*)

AN COILEACHAN

3028ft/923m The cockerel or little cock

Despite its distribution in the Scottish hills there are few hill names which suggest an abundance of grouse. This hill may be one if only as a foreshortened version of 'coileach ruadh', the red cock.

As the first mountain encountered on the private estate road into Fannich Lodge the mountain is a true clarion of the mountain day yet to come.

Below: An Coileachan from the road to Fannich Lodge (*John Allen*)

BEINN LIATH MHOR FANNAICH

3130ft/954m Big grey mountain of Fannich

As the biggest hill in the Fannaich range possessing scree in any quantity this aspect of the hill was chosen to distinguish it by name.

This peak suffers from its proximity to a dominant Sgurr Mor. Ridge walkers attempting the grand traverse of the Fannichs find the diversion to its unprepossessing cairn, and the consequent re-ascent to the main ridge, does little to enhance its popularity.

Above: Beinn Liath Mhor Fannaich from Sgurr Mor (*Alan O'Brien*)

MEALL GORM

3113ft/949m Blue hill

The word 'meall' in the name suggests this is a rounded hill. The blue here is blue-green from the grass as the grassiest slopes of the Fannichs lie here and as such would be noted by those who lived below as a source of good pasturage.

Its broad ridge links the eastern and central Fannich summits and as such helps speed progress on many a mountain circuit in this range as well as adding its own summit to the tally of Munros.

Left: Meall Gorm from Sgurr Mor (*Jim Teesdale*)

FIONN BHEINN

3061ft/933m The white mountain

The colour of the moss-grass on this hill's slopes above Achnasheen stand in contrast to the stark moors which surround it. The term white here is intended to imply a light coloured hill. This would be more apparent in an area subjected to the prevailing westerly winds as the colours can appear much richer in the clearer atmosphere produced by sunlight and showers.

The ease of ascent from Achnasheen makes this a perfect hill for the short winter's day with ample time to sit at the summit, an ideal view-point to sample views of the hills of Torridon, Fisherfield, Fannich and those of Strath Conon across the long sweep of Strath Bran to the east.

Right: Looking south-east from Fionn Bheinn (*Alan O'Brien*)

CONA' MHEALL

3215ft/980m Adjoining hill

Origins of this hill name are obscure and the most likely explanation is that the name is taken from the Gaelic 'con' meaning together, or with, and 'mheall' a hill. The significance is that here this mountain has the appearance of being a shoulder of another peak, in this case Beinn Dearg. The word 'con' is most often associated with dogs, and is often more readily accepted in translation. Here it is a less reliable interpretation, as there are no other hills close with names to suggest links with hunting.

BEINN DEARG

3556ft/1084m Red mountain

Heather gives this hill its redness and to differentiate between it and other mountains of the same name it is often referred to as the Ullapool Beinn Dearg as it forms a substantial part of that township's eastern horizon.

Set some distance from the road these mountains conceal from view the loch of an eastern corrie. This is Coire Granda, the ugly corrie, the raw womb cradled by these guardian heights.

Right: Beinn Dearg and Cona' Mheall from Dirrie More (*Irvine Butterfield*)

BEN WYVIS - GLAS LEATHAD MOR

3432ft/1046m Awesome mountain – Big greenish-grey slope

The massive flank which bulks large above the Garve-Ullapool road is truly awesome and this seems the most appropriate origin of the mountain's name from the now obsolete Gaelic 'fuathais', a great quantity. The greenish-grey colouring results from the springs which darken the grassy flanks.

The mountain heaves its great bulk above the surrounding forest along the Ullapool road, its great whaleback the one horizon seen on the eastwards crossing of a distant watershed of the Dirrie More.

Above: Ben Wyvis from Carn na Dubh Choille (*Jim Teesdale*)

AM FAOCHAGACH

3130ft/954m The heathery place

As the mountain's lower slopes are thick with heather and bilberry the Am Fraochagach of former mapping better describes the mountain as the heathery or berried place. Its landlocked situation does not quite equate to a place of shells which the other interpretation, whelk-shaped mountain, suggests.

Hill-walkers tend to neglect this hill. Its reputation goes before it as a long tedious drag of heathered humps and excites little praise even from the most ardent baggers.

Right: Am Faochagach from Strath Vaich (*Irvine Butterfield*)

MEALL NAN CEAPRAICHEAN

3205ft/977m Hill of the little tops

The literal translation of the hill of stubby hillocks well describes the summit of this mountain which is a stony plain possessing several tumuli-like tops.

Surveyed from nearby Eididh nan Clach Geala, the mountain's rounded cap might well be dismissed as little more than a stepping stone to the great dome of Beinn Dearg beyond.

Above left: Meall nan Ceapraichean and Beinn Dearg from Eididh nan Clach Geala (*Jim Teesdale*)

EIDIDH NAN CLACH GEALA

3044ft/928m Web of white stones

The fractured quartzite rocks capping this hill must have suggested an intricate pattern to those who saw the summit. Those with a perceptive eye will well appreciate the romantic vision of those who named it. In common with its neighbour, a slope facing Gleann na Sguaib possesses buttressing crag in contrast to a rounded summit. The view from the summit of one to the other gives little hint of the divide between, though this is more appreciable between the southern height and its other neighbour, Beinn Dearg.

Below left: Eididh nan Clach Geala from Meall nan Ceapraichean (*Jim Teesdale*)

SEANA BHRAIGH

3041ft/927m Old height

It is difficult to come up with a plausible explanation for this hill's name unless it is something to do with the wrinkling of the schists exposed on the great face of a dramatic northern cliff above the deep cauldron of the Luchd Choire. Across this impressive hollow a second plunge wall falls to the twinned pools of a loch, and it is this view which holds in thrall all who see it.

Right: Creag an Duine from the summit of Seana Bhraigh (*Alan O'Brien*)

BEN MORE ASSYNT

3274ft/998m Great mountain of Assynt

This is one mountain with a Norse-Gaelic hybrid name, Assynt being a derivative of the Norse 'ass', a rocky ridge. Those who visit its summit find the ridge is indeed rocky and as the highest mountain in the district it affords a fine view-point.

CONIVAL

3238ft/987m Adjoining hill

Some say this is the enchanted hill but like the hill of similar name to the south it is more like a shoulder of a great sprawl of hill, here The Great Mountain of Assynt. Otherwise stick with derivation from 'con' – a dog!

The two hills are a formidable barrier whose melting snows feed an infant River Oykel. The two are best seen from the western wall of the glen carved by the river with the origins of their names well demonstrated by size and proximity one to the other.

Above left: Conival and Ben More Assynt from Breabag (*Jim Teesdale*)

BEN HOPE

3041ft/927m Mountain of the bay

The Norse 'hop', a bay, lends its name to this hill which to the Scandinavian sea-raiders stood as a landmark between the sea-lanes of Loch Eriboll and the Kyle of Tongue.

As a singular mountain it is easily identified from the other Sutherland hills. From hills such as Ben loyal it appears as a long crouched hump.

Below left: Ben Hope from Ben Loyal (*Iain A. Robertson*)

BEN KLIBRECK

3156ft/962m Mountain of the speckled cliff

The letter 'k' in the mountain's name and its location in north-west Sutherland indicates a Norse connection, probably 'clete' or 'klif brekka', the cliff slope, which, given a steep northern slope broken with outcrops, would have been familiar to Norse raiders pushing into the country from the northern sea lochs.

Looking across a once populous Strath Naver the settlers would have first seen a view which has a timeless quality.

Right: Ben Klibreck from Strath Naver (*Irvine Butterfield*)

THE ISLANDS

SKYE OF THE JAGGED PEAKS AND SHARP *ARÊTES* IS THE TRUE MECCA OF THE mountaineer for these are without doubt the most rugged and awe-inspiring peaks in Britain. Here many of the hills lacked title until the early rock climbers took it upon themselves to celebrate their earliest conquests. The Cuillin are the haunt of the cragsman, and to the ardent Munroist provide the ultimate test on the narrow flake of the Inaccessible Pinnacle.

Right: Inaccessible Pinnacle (*Paul Craven*)

BEN MORE (MULL)

3169ft/966m Big mountain

As the highest mountain in Mull and one of ample girth it simply attracted the most obvious appellation; it is a big mountain in every sense.

The ascent might be little more than the continuous pull from the road alongside Loch na Keal but this would be to ignore an opportunity to make the most of the day by traversing the lesser satellite of A'Chioch either in ascent or descent.

Left: Ascending the east ridge of Ben More (*Ralph Storer*)

SGURR NAN GILLEAN

3163ft/964m Peak of the young men

Norse influences may also have equal validity here as their word 'gil', meaning a ghyll or gully, is well represented on the lacerated faces of this majestic peak and its attendant Pinnacle Ridge.

For the majority of mountaineers this is their first introduction to the great peaks of Skye. Standing beside the burn at Sligachan it is easy to understand why the redoubtable Dr Norman Collie, pioneer of so many of the rock climbs and after whom Sgurr Thormaid is named, made the hotel his home in his later years so that he might be near his beloved Cuillin.

Right: Sgurr nan Gillean from Sligachan (*Ian Evans*)

AM BASTEIR

3064ft/934m The executioner

The adjacent Bhasteir Tooth bears some resemblance to an axe hence the acceptance of the Gaelic 'basadair', executioner, as the likely source of the name. The name might equally be a corrupt derivation of 'baisteach', a baptiser, as the tooth from a distance has the appearance of the bent head of a cowled priest.

Left: Sgurr a' Fionn Choire and Am Basteir from Sgurr nan Gillean (*John Allen*)

BRUACH NA FRITHE

3143ft/958m Slope of the deer-forest

Of all the Cuillin peaks this is the one which best describes the area, for the Gaelic 'frith' also means wilderness and who would dispute the wild and grand scene as witnessed from its summit, rightly regarded as one of the finest viewpoints in the range.

Right: Bruach na Frithe looking south to the Dubhs ridge (*Jim Teesdale*)

SGURR DUBH MOR

3097ft/944m Big black peak

The name of this mountain might have been applied to any of the Cuillin, some of which are higher. Sited just off the main ridge-line it probably attracted more attention and hence was named before most of the others.

The finest ascent lies by the Dubhs' Ridge which climbs from Loch Coruisk where slabs provide the first of many rocky stairways to the summit turret.

Below: On the Dubhs' Ridge (*Lorraine Nicholson*)

SGURR A' MHADAIDH (SOUTH-WEST TOP)

3012ft/918m Peak of the fox

There must have been fox dens on this mountain and Reynard would have ample choice of sites among the boulder-strewn ridges and summit. An access gully climbing from Tairneilar known as the Foxes' Rake was one of the traditional scrambling routes to the summit.

Another route by way of Sgurr Thuilm provides a route free of the technical difficulties encountered on the traverse of the main ridge.

Above: Sgurr a' Mhadaidh from Sgurr Thuilm (*John Allen*)

SGURR A' GHREADAIDH

3192ft/973m Peak of the thrashing
Various explanations have been put
forward to account for this peak's
association with whipping, torment or
anxiety. The most colourful relates to a
cruel tradition when the marking of clan
boundaries was accompanied by the severe
beating of a young boy from each of the
clans represented, so that they would
forever remember where the exact
boundary markers were. Climbers
approaching the narrow blade of the
summit ridge will be more mindful of
other suggestions that the thrashing
might be that of the mighty winds which
buffet its exposed battlement. Guardian
rocks set like teeth on the ridge from
Sgurr Thormaid, and the rising *arête*
beyond, are precursors to the most finely
honed crest in the Cuillin.

Left: Sgurr a' Ghreadaidh from Sgurr
Thormaid (*John Allen*)

SGURR ALASDAIR

3254ft/992m Peak of Alexander (Nicolson)
This, the highest of the Cuillin, and by
many considered the most elegant of the
many spires in the range, was named after
Skye's own Sheriff Alexander Nicolson,
another of the early pioneers of Cuillin
exploration, who made the first ascent.

Partnered with this great peak is the
classic route by way of the Great Stone
Chute which from neighbouring
belvederes may seem almost vertical.
Left: Sgurr Alasdair from the foot of An
Stac (*Irvine Butterfield*)

SGURR NA BANACHDICH (NORTH TOP)

3166ft/965m Peak of the smallpox

Banachaig, a dairy maid, could be a likely connection with this mountain as in days past there were hill shielings on the peak's western slopes and it was customary for the young girls to attend there for the milking. Locally the interpretation is smallpox peak which is supported by reference to the pitted appearance of the mountain. Though less romantic this seems the most reliable explanation.

SGURR DEARG – INACCESSIBLE PINNACLE

3235ft/986m Red peak

The reddish hue of the rocks is an obvious contender for the peak's name. The pinnacle overtops the main summit and was considered unscaleable until the brothers Charles and Laurence Pilkington made an ascent by its long eastern edge on 18 August 1880. It was to remain one of the few summits that Munro himself did not attain.

Speak of the Cuillin and it is almost taken for granted that mist will feature in the conversation. Its vapours do not last for ever and as their curtain rises from a chosen summit there is much expectation that this may herald the opening performance of a fine day.

Above right: Sgurr Dearg from the summit of Sgurr na Banachdich (*John Allen*)

SGURR NAN EAG

3031ft/924m Peak of the notches

Sometimes erroneously called horses' peak its name is taken from the gap in the ridge between Coir' a' Ghrunnda and An Garbh-choire.

The view across the head of Coir' a' Ghrunnda best portrays the mountain's situation close to the end of the ridge. As a classic view unlikely to be equalled it is worthy of inclusion in these mountain views.

Left: Sgurr nan Eag from Sgurr Alasdair (*John Allen*)

SGURR MHIC CHOINNICH

3110ft/948m MacKenzie's peak

This magnificent peak on the headwall of
Coire Lagan was jokingly named Pic
Mhic Choinnich by Charles Pilkington
after the guide and gillie John MacKenzie
who accompanied many of the early
pioneers. The name stuck but the Gaelic
'sgurr' was the preferred rendition of the
word for peak as a tribute to a man
regarded as the first Cuillin guide.

Right: Sgurr Mhic Choinnich from Sgurr
Thearlaich (*John Allen*)

BLA BHEINN

3044ft/928m Mountain of bloom

This hill name could be a mix of the Old Norse 'bla', meaning blue, and the popular Gaelic word for a hill 'bheinn', though people tend to hold strictly to the Gaelic 'blath bheinn', mountain of bloom.

The commanding height of Bla Bheinn rises fully 3000ft from the sea. Linked to the craggy Clach Glas it provides one of the grandest mountain traverses in Britain and to those who come to know them the two are inextricably linked. In the photographic sense whatever time of day is chosen the pair are an imposing backdrop to the waters of Loch Slapin.

Left: Bla Bheinn and Clach Glas from Torrin (*Irvine Butterfield*)

191

INDEX